Chow Baby!

THE TRAVELER'S GUIDE

TO CHEAP, HEALTHY COOKING

BY MIKE HEDLEY

THE MOUNTAINEERS BOOKS
*is the nonprofit publishing arm of The Mountaineers Club, an
organization founded in 1906 and dedicated to the exploration,
preservation, and enjoyment of outdoor and wilderness areas.*

1001 SW Klickitat Way, Suite 201, Seattle, WA 98134

© 2006 by Mike Hedley

First edition 2006

Manufactured in the United States of America

Acquiring Editor: Cassandra Conyers
Developmental Editor: Janet Kimball
Project Editor: Margaret Sullivan
Copy Editor: Kris Fulsaas
Design and layout: Karen Schober Book Design
Cover and Interior Illustration: Tracy Daberko
All photographs by the author unless otherwise noted.

A catalog record is on file at the Library of Congress.

Printed on recycled paper

Dedicated to, and inspired by, the adventurers of the world

Contents

———

INTRODUCTION

It all started with a package of ramen noodles. I was a few months into what was to become a two-year backpacking adventure through Australia, New Zealand, Thailand, and Germany. I had begun to notice that my fellow travelers either subsisted on a diet of ramen ("two-minute") noodles, canned pastas, and other unhealthy convenience foods or they ate out in restaurants, spending much of their travel budget on food. One evening in a hostel kitchen in Australia, I watched a woman add fresh vegetables to her ramen noodles in an attempt to make the noodles more nutritious, even if not much tastier. I thought, "Why don't I take this to a whole new level?" I figured I could use my background as a chef and my experience as a traveler to create simple recipes for travelers that taste great and are also much healthier.

So as I traveled for the next two years, I developed an extensive repertoire of healthy recipes that incorporate inexpensive, easy-to-find ingredients in creative ways, allowing travelers to eat well and save their money for their adventures. This book includes my 50 favorite recipes, grouped in sections by meal type (breakfast, lunch, dinner, etc.). They've been tested and tasted many times by anyone who happened to share a kitchen with me in hostels around the world. Whether you are staying in hostels, renting a house or an apartment, or traveling in a recreational vehicle, you'll be able to use this book to prepare simple, delicious meals.

Though none of the recipes are difficult, I've organized them within each section starting from the least expensive and easiest to those that are just a bit more complicated. All the ingredients should be easy to find in the most commonly traveled countries around the world. I also offer lots of ideas for substitutions and variations so you can adjust any of the recipes to suit your tastes or to incorporate what is readily available in local markets. None of the measurements need to be very precise, so if the kitchen you are using isn't very well equipped, there's no need to give up on cooking. Just use the recipes as a guideline and be creative. You might be surprised by the food you can create, even if you don't consider yourself much of a cook.

Cooking while traveling, as opposed to always eating in restaurants, offers many wonderful benefits. Not only will you save money and eat more healthfully, you will also find that shopping for ingredients gives you the perfect excuse to dive into local culture. Small towns in particular come alive on market days, allowing you to experience sights, sounds, and a sense of community that will add new depth to your travel experiences. Even if you don't speak the language, you'll probably be able to purchase what you need. If you are unfamiliar with an area's shopping protocol, just take a few minutes to observe what the locals do. Do they touch the produce, or do they allow the vendor to make their selections? Do they wait in line, or do you need to jump in and get the vendor's attention? If you are patient and willing to do some pointing or use some creative sign language, you'll find that shopping in a different country can be one of the most enjoyable parts of your travels.

I have a vivid memory of a day in a small coastal town in Australia when my girlfriend was preparing to return home while I continued my travels. We wanted to prepare a special dinner, so we spent hours wandering the local market and enjoying the day, selecting prawns, tomatoes, fresh basil, and cheeses. Returning to the hostel, we cooked together, making garlic prawns, Summer Fresh Tomato-Basil Salad, and Blue Cheese Smashed Potatoes (see Salads and Side Dishes). It was a day and a dinner to remember, and I think even the fanciest local restaurant couldn't have competed with the wonderful experience we had.

If you are staying in a place where the kitchen is shared, you'll find that cooking is an excellent way to meet fellow travelers. Some of the recipes in this book are meant for a group, and there's no better way to make new friends than to cook up a batch of chili or a big lasagna. One of my favorite travel memories is of an evening in Byron Bay, Australia, when a group of us made some Pasta Bolognese (see Dinner) together. Matt chopped the vegetables, Eric boiled the pasta, Katie set the table, Glen poured the drinks, and I livened up the sauce with a few dashes of red wine. We had a fantastic time cooking together and sharing that meal, and in the end it cost each of us just a few dollars.

One of my primary reasons for creating this book was to help travelers eat well to stay healthy. After all, you can't enjoy your travels if you aren't properly fueling your body, and you really can't enjoy your adventures if you get sick. In my view, a healthy diet is quite simple. It should be low in saturated fats, and you should get as many vitamins and minerals as possible from fresh foods. You also need to consume some protein at every meal, which can come from red meat, fish, chicken, tofu, eggs, yogurt, cheese, whole grains, green leafy vegetables, beans and legumes, nuts, nut butters, or seeds. The key is to balance nutrients by eating a variety of foods. A sample daily menu could be this: Backpacker's Muesli for breakfast, a Veggie Wrap (see Sandwiches, Wraps, and Snacks) for lunch, and the Mixed Vegetable Stir-Fry, Hearty Chili, or Pasta Olio for dinner. You simply need to keep your foods in balance. If you are a vegetarian, you can easily replace any meat in the recipes with tofu or a vegetarian meat substitute, but you should try to get protein from a wide variety of sources.

I encourage you to use these recipes as a base for experimentation. Try the variations or follow your own inspiration. If you keep fresh vegetables on hand, you'll always be able to come up with a healthy pizza, wrap, stir-fry, melt, pasta, or salad. I never went anywhere without salsa and sweet chili sauce. They make excellent emergency substitutes for salad dressings or add extra zip to melts, sandwiches, and wraps. If you put a little bit of extra effort into shopping and preparing healthy food, you'll make your travels more fun and less expensive, and you'll open yourself up to some great new experiences. Bon appetit and bon voyage!

Breakfast

BACKPACKER'S MUESLI

Makes 2 servings

Muesli is an excellent breakfast choice when you are on the go. Not only is it inexpensive and healthy, it will also keep your hunger satisfied nearly all day. This is my favorite flavor combination, but you can use any fruit and any yogurt flavors. I also like grapefruit, bananas, and oranges with citrus-flavored yogurt or a mix of fresh berries with any berry-flavored yogurt.

½ cup (125 ml) peeled, seeded, and diced cantaloupe (also known as rockmelon)
½ cup (125 ml) peeled, seeded, and diced honeydew melon
½ cup (125 ml) blueberries
6 strawberries, halved
2 cups (500 ml) rolled oats, granola, or plain muesli
½ cup (125 ml) mixed berry yogurt

In a small bowl, stir together the fruit, rolled oats (or granola or muesli), and yogurt.

Note: Store leftover fruit in the refrigerator in an airtight container; it will keep for up to one week.

Variation: Substitute dried fruit for the fresh fruit. Dried cranberries, raisins, dates, sultans, and apricots are delicious when mixed with muesli and yogurt.

BREAKFAST SANDWICH

Makes 2 sandwiches

*A sandwich is an easy and satisfying start to the day.
It could be something as simple as peanut butter and banana
slices on toast. Or you can cook a couple slices of bacon for a bacon,
lettuce, and tomato sandwich—a BLT. If you have a little more time,
try this breakfast sandwich. I like it with a fried egg, but you
can prepare the egg any way you wish.*

2 tablespoons (30 ml) canola oil
6 to 8 thin slices green bell pepper
4 mushrooms, washed and thinly sliced
2 eggs
4 pieces whole grain bread, toasted
2 tablespoons (30 ml) barbecue sauce, divided
6 slices tomato
4 to 6 thin slices Cheddar cheese
Salt and pepper, to taste

1. Heat the oil in a small skillet over medium-high heat. Add the peppers and mushrooms and cook, stirring frequently, about one minute or until tender. Remove the vegetables from the pan and set aside.

2. Return the skillet to medium-high heat. Crack the eggs into the pan. Cook for one to two minutes, or until the yolks begin to firm up and the egg whites are almost completely opaque. With a rubber spatula, gently flip each egg over and continue cooking for another two minutes, or until the yolks are cooked to your preference.

3. While the eggs are cooking, toast the bread. Spread a tablespoon (15 ml) of barbecue sauce on two slices of toast and top with the cooked vegetables, tomato slices, cheese, and cooked egg. Season to taste and cover with the other two slices of toast. If the cheese doesn't melt enough, heat the sandwiches in a microwave for 10 to 15 seconds.

Variation: Substitute salsa, ketchup, or steak sauce for the barbecue sauce.

HASH BROWNS

Makes 4 to 5 servings

I have worked in restaurants all over the world, and I have made hash browns in many of them. Everyone seems to love them when they're eating in restaurants, but they never make them at home. This recipe shows you how easy they are. Note that the cooked potatoes need to cool for at least two hours before you fry them. I like to boil the potatoes in the evening while I'm preparing dinner, then they're ready to go first thing in the morning. This is a larger recipe, which is perfect for a group breakfast. Or you can store the boiled potatoes in the refrigerator and make the hash browns in small batches over the course of a week.

4 large baking potatoes, washed
⅓ cup (75 ml) canola oil, divided
1 large yellow onion, peeled and finely sliced, about 2 cups (500 ml)
Salt and pepper, to taste

1. Place the potatoes in a pot of salted water, making sure the water covers the potatoes by at least 3 inches (7.5 cm). Cover and bring to a boil over high heat. Uncover and reduce the heat to medium-low. Simmer for about 15 to 20 minutes, checking the potatoes for doneness after 10 minutes. The potatoes are done when easily pierced by a fork.

2. Drain the water from the pot and allow the potatoes to cool. Do not run cold water over them because that will make them soggy. When the potatoes are no longer steaming, place them uncovered in the refrigerator and cool completely. (This may take up to two hours.)

3. Cut the cooled potatoes into ½-inch (1-cm) bite-size pieces. You'll have about 4 to 5 cups of chopped potatoes.

4. Heat 3 to 4 tablespoons (45 to 60 ml) of the vegetable oil in a large skillet over high heat. Cooking in batches, add half the potatoes to the skillet and cook, stirring occasionally, for four or five minutes or until the potatoes are golden brown on all sides.

5. Add 1 cup (250 ml) of the sliced onions and cook, stirring occasionally, for two or three minutes or until the onions are soft and translucent. Season well with salt and pepper, then transfer the hash browns onto a plate lined with a paper towel to absorb any extra oil.

6. Add 3 to 4 more tablespoons (45 to 60 ml) oil to the pan and repeat steps 4 and 5 with the remaining potatoes and onions.

Variations

1. In step 4, add ½ cup (125 ml) finely sliced cooked sausage to the skillet along with the potatoes.

2. In step 5, add ½ cup (125 ml) of finely diced ham, chopped cooked bacon, sliced mushrooms, or diced bell pepper along with the onions.

FRENCH TOAST

Makes 2 servings

I didn't make French toast very often until I met a group of French Canadian travelers in the Rocky Mountains who made it every morning. They always added extra cinnamon to the egg mixture and topped off the toast with maple syrup and apple preserves. It gave me a new appreciation for the versatility of French toast and inspired me to come up with some simple variations of my own.

2 large eggs
½ cup (125 ml) milk
1 teaspoon (5 ml) cinnamon
1 teaspoon (5 ml) salt
2 tablespoons (30 ml) vegetable oil
4 slices multigrain bread

1. Crack the eggs into a bowl. Add the milk, cinnamon, and salt. Beat with a fork or whisk until combined.

2. Heat the oil in a small skillet over medium heat. Dip the bread into the egg mixture, coating both sides. Transfer the bread to the hot skillet and cook until golden brown on one side. Flip with a spatula and brown the other side. Serve immediately with maple syrup, corn syrup, peanut butter, or fresh fruit.

Variations

1. Citrus French Toast: For a zesty option, grate 2 tablespoons (30 ml) lemon or orange rind into the egg mixture.

2. Irish Toast: Replace the ½ cup (125 ml) milk with ½ cup (125 ml) Irish cream–flavored coffee cream and add 2 teaspoons (10 ml) granulated sugar to the egg mixture.

3. Hazelnut French Toast: Replace the $\frac{1}{2}$ cup (125 ml) milk with $\frac{1}{2}$ cup (125 ml) hazelnut-flavored coffee cream and add $\frac{1}{2}$ teaspoon (2 ml) nutmeg to the egg mixture.

4. Party French Toast: Use only $\frac{1}{4}$ cup (60 ml) milk and add $\frac{1}{4}$ cup (60 ml) coffee-flavored liqueur or Irish cream–flavored coffee cream to the egg mixture.

PANCAKES

Makes 2 servings

I once worked at a hostel in Darwin, Australia, paying for my accommodations by making the other backpackers a pancake breakfast buffet. It was much appreciated by the backpackers, and I learned that anything goes regarding pancake toppings—especially maple syrup. Even if you've never made pancakes from scratch before, try these. Once you make your own, you'll never go back to pancake mix again.

1 cup (250 ml) all-purpose flour
1 teaspoon (5 ml) baking powder
1 teaspoon (5 ml) granulated sugar
$\frac{1}{4}$ teaspoon (1 ml) salt
1 egg
1 cup (250 ml) milk
2 tablespoons (30 ml) vegetable or canola oil, divided

1. Combine the flour, baking powder, sugar, and salt in a medium-size bowl. Crack the egg into the bowl, add the milk, and beat the mixture with a fork or a whisk until it is smooth and without lumps.

2. Heat ½ tablespoon (7 ml) of the oil in a nonstick skillet over medium heat. Add ¼ cup (60 ml) of pancake batter for each pancake, cooking in batches and adding more oil as necessary for each batch. Cook each pancake for two to three minutes on the first side or until golden brown, then flip with a spatula and cook until the other side is golden brown. Serve immediately.

Variation: After the batter is thoroughly mixed, gently fold in ¼ cup (60 ml) blueberries or diced banana and proceed as directed in step 2.

BREAKFAST BURRITO

Makes 2 burritos

This recipe has always been one of my favorites, especially on days when I'm heading out on a road trip early in the morning. Just wrap it in a napkin, and you're ready to go—no plates to wash! These are very adaptable to whatever ingredients you have on hand.

2 tablespoons (30 ml) canola oil
½ cup (125 ml) diced uncooked bacon (optional)
½ cup (125ml) peeled and chopped yellow onion
2 large eggs
1½ scant tablespoons (20 ml) taco or burrito seasoning (see Note)
Salt and pepper, to taste
¼ cup (60mL) canned baked beans
½ cup (125 ml) diced tomato
2 flour tortillas
2 tablespoons (30 ml) salsa, divided
½ cup (125 ml) shredded Cheddar cheese, divided

1. Heat the oil in a skillet over medium heat. When the oil is hot, add the bacon (if using) and sauté for one minute. Add the onions and cook, stirring frequently, for about one to two minutes or until they are soft and translucent.

2. Add the eggs, taco or burrito seasoning, salt, and pepper. Cook, stirring frequently, for another minute or until the eggs are just cooked. Stir in the baked beans and tomato and cook until warm (about one minute).

3. Heat the tortillas in a microwave for 10 to 15 seconds. Spread half the salsa over each tortilla, all the way to the edges. Place half the egg mixture down the center of each tortilla, top each tortilla with half the cheese, then fold each tortilla over the ends of the egg mixture before rolling it up.

Note: Taco or burrito seasoning is usually easy to find, but if it's not, substitute 1 teaspoon (5 ml) *each* cumin and ground coriander.

Variations

1. Substitute diced deli-style ham for the bacon and add it in step 3 with the cheese.

2. Cheese Egg Burrito: For an even simpler burrito, just scramble one egg and 1 tablespoon (15 ml) salsa in a hot skillet. Wrap the egg mixture in a warm flour tortilla with a good pinch of your favorite grated cheese.

3. Sausage Egg Burrito: Dice one large lean uncooked sausage link. Add the diced sausage to the skillet with the onion in step 1 and proceed as directed. You can substitute the sausage for the bacon or use both.

SPINACH AND TOMATO FRITTATA

Makes 2 servings

You can put almost anything into a frittata.
Try adding ham, cooked bacon, broccoli, eggplant, or zucchini, or
toss in a pinch of basil or oregano. If you like your vegetables crunchy,
just add them to the egg mixture in step 1. If you prefer them tender,
see Variation 2: Sautéed Vegetable Frittata. Serve the frittata
warm for breakfast, or pack it in acooler and serve
it cold for a picnic lunch.

6 eggs
1 tablespoon (15 ml) milk
$\frac{1}{2}$ cup (125 ml) thinly sliced spinach leaves
$\frac{1}{2}$ cup (125 ml) diced tomato
Salt and pepper, to taste
1 tablespoon (15 ml) butter or vegetable oil
$\frac{1}{2}$ cup (125 ml) grated Parmesan cheese

1. Preheat the broiler.

2. In a medium-size bowl, whisk together the eggs, milk, spinach, tomato, salt, and pepper.

3. Heat the butter or vegetable oil in a large nonstick skillet over medium heat. Pour the egg mixture into the pan (do not stir) and reduce the heat to very low. Cook until the egg mixture has thickened and set and is creamy only in the center of the pan.

4. Sprinkle the cheese over the egg mixture and transfer the skillet to the top rack of an oven set to broil. As soon as the surface of the frittata has set and the cheese is melted, remove the skillet from the oven and serve immediately.

Variations

1. Asparagus Parmesan Frittata: Substitute ½ cup (125 ml) chopped and cooked asparagus for the spinach. Before step 1, bring 2 to 3 cups (500 to 750 ml) water to boil in a small saucepan. Add the asparagus and cook for one to two minutes or until just lightly cooked but still a bit firm. Drain in a colander, then run cold water over the asparagus until cool. Add the asparagus to the egg mixture in step 1 and proceed as directed. (This method can also be used for any vegetable you'd rather blanch than sauté.)

2. Sautéed Vegetable Frittata: Substitute ½ cup (125 ml) each of two diced and cooked vegetables of your choice for the spinach: bell pepper, zucchini, yellow onion, broccoli, eggplant, or mushrooms. Before step 1, heat the oil in the skillet over medium heat. Add the diced vegetables and cook, stirring occasionally, for one to two minutes or until the vegetables are tender. Then proceed as directed in step 1. In step 2, pour the egg mixture into the skillet with the sautéed vegetables and proceed as directed.

EASY OMELET

Makes 2 servings

Omelets are excellent travelers' fare because the ingredients—eggs, vegetables, and cheese—are readily available almost anywhere. This recipe is for a Canadian omelet, but you can vary the fillings endlessly. The key to making a good omelet is an unscratched nonstick skillet. Select the best-quality skillet you can find. I once hid a pan on my food shelf because it was such a nice one.

*But I don't condone that kind of behavior! And I did share my
omelet . . . . This recipe makes a big omelet, so cut the omelet in half and
share with a friend, or share with a stranger and make a new friend!*

4 large eggs
2 tablespoons (30 ml) milk
Salt and pepper, to taste
2 tablespoons (30 ml) canola oil, butter, or margarine
2 tablespoons (30 ml) finely diced tomato
¹/₄ cup (60 ml) diced ham
¹/₄ cup (60 ml) shredded Cheddar cheese

1. Crack the eggs into a bowl. Add the milk, salt, and pepper, and beat with a fork or a whisk until the milk and eggs are combined and smooth.

2. Heat the oil, butter, or margarine in a nonstick skillet over medium-high heat. Add the egg mixture, pouring slowly in a circular motion around the pan. When all the egg mixture is in the pan, tilt the pan back and forth to make sure the egg mixture evenly covers the bottom of the pan and there are no holes in the egg mixture.

3. Sprinkle the tomato, ham, and cheese over half the egg surface and continue cooking without stirring. When the egg mixture is cooked through and is no longer runny, use a spatula to fold half the omelet over the side with the filling. Flip the folded omelet over as needed to complete cooking and heat through.

Filling Variations

1. Vegetarian Florentine Omelet: 10 to 12 spinach leaves, washed and dried; 1 tablespoon (15 ml) chopped chives; ¹/₄ teaspoon (1 ml) dried oregano or basil.

2. Spring Omelet: 1 2-ounce (57-g) piece smoked salmon, sliced; ¼ cup (60 ml) diced Brie cheese; 2 tablespoons (30 ml) chopped chives.

SAUTÉED VEGETABLE OMELET

Makes 2 servings

Wander an outdoor market in the afternoon and seek out the freshest in-season vegetables you can find. This recipe is simply a guideline; any vegetables will do. In the morning you'll have the makings for this healthy and satisfying omelet. Make your coffee while the vegetables are cooking, and in minutes you can enjoy a nice, hot breakfast.

4 large eggs, divided
2 tablespoons (30 ml) milk, divided
Salt and pepper, to taste
4 tablespoons (60 ml) canola oil, butter, or margarine, divided
2 large mushrooms, washed and sliced
¼ cup (60 ml) diced red onion
¼ cup (60 ml) diced bell pepper

1. Crack the eggs into a bowl. Add the milk, salt, and pepper and beat with a fork or a whisk until the milk and eggs are combined and smooth.

2. Heat 2 tablespoons (30 ml) of the oil, butter, or margarine in a small skillet over medium-high heat. Add the mushrooms, onion, and peppers to the skillet and cook, stirring

occasionally, for two to three minutes or until tender. Remove the vegetables from the pan and set aside.

3. Heat 1 tablespoon (15 ml) of the oil, butter, or margarine in the skillet over medium-high heat. Add half the egg mixture, pouring slowly in a circular motion around the pan. Tilt the pan back and forth to make sure the egg mixture evenly covers the bottom of the pan and there are no holes in the egg mixture.

4. Sprinkle half the sautéed vegetables over half the egg surface and continue cooking without stirring. When the egg mixture is cooked through and is no longer runny, use a spatula to fold half the omelet over the side with the filling. Flip the folded omelet over as needed to complete cooking and heat through. Serve immediately.

5. Repeat steps 3 and 4 for the second omelet.

Variations

Replace any of the vegetables with any of the following for each omelet:

2 tablespoons (30 ml) diced zucchini

2 tablespoons (30 ml) diced eggplant

2 tablespoons (30 ml) diced green onion

2 tablespoons (30 ml) diced ham or cooked bacon

Sandwiches, Wraps, and Snacks

BASIC SAUTÉED CHICKEN

Makes 2 servings

*You can use Basic Sautéed Chicken in any
number of ways. Add the chicken from this recipe to the Vegetable
Quesadilla or Bean and Vegetable Burrito (both in this chapter),
Pizza (see Dinner), or Pasta Salad (see Salads and Side Dishes).
Wrap it up in a flour tortilla along with some cucumber, shredded
Cheddar cheese, and salsa for a delicious, healthy, and fast
lunch, as in the Veggie Wrap (in this chapter).*

2 chicken breasts, chopped into bite-size pieces
2 teaspoons (10 ml) minced garlic (about 2 to 4 cloves),
    or 2 teaspoons (10 ml) garlic powder
1 teaspoon (5 ml) Italian herb mix, or 1 teaspoon
    (5 ml) total dried oregano, basil, and thyme
2 teaspoons (10 ml) fresh lemon juice
Salt and pepper, to taste
2 tablespoons (30 ml) vegetable oil
2 tablespoons (30 ml) white wine (optional)

1. In a bowl, combine the chicken, garlic, Italian herb mix,
lemon juice, salt, and pepper.

2. Heat the oil in a small skillet over medium heat. When
the oil is hot, add the chicken mixture to the pan and cook, stirring occasionally, for five to six minutes or until the outside of
the chicken is no longer pink. Add the white wine (if using) and
continue cooking until the chicken is no longer pink in the middle. Serve the chicken on a salad, in a wrap, or on top of the pasta
of your choice.

Variations

Substitute 1 teaspoon (5 ml) of any of the following herbs or spices in place of the Italian herb mix:

Dried basil
Chili powder
Chopped fresh cilantro
Cumin
Lemon pepper
Mexican spice mix
Oregano
Thyme

VEGGIE WRAP

Makes 2 wraps

When you are looking for a quick, healthy lunch, you'll find that wraps have infinite possibilities. You can use this recipe as a base and go from there. Replace the salsa with barbecue sauce, sweet chili sauce, or pesto for new flavors. Add leftover chicken or steak, or add some sliced deli meats to bump up the protein of your wrap. For a salad on the go, wrap up some Curried Eggs (in this chapter), Asian Beef Salad, or Taco Salad (both in Salads and Side Dishes).

2 cups (500 ml) shredded lettuce
1/4 cup (60 ml) diced tomato
1/4 cup (60 ml) shredded carrot
4 slices red onion
2 tablespoons (30 ml) peeled and diced cucumber
1/2 cup (125 ml) alfalfa sprouts

2 flour tortillas

2 heaping tablespoons (30 ml) salsa, divided

½ cup (125 ml) shredded Cheddar cheese, divided

1. Combine the lettuce, tomato, carrot, onion, cucumber, and sprouts in a bowl.

2. Heat the tortillas in a microwave for 10 to 20 seconds or until just warm.

3. Spread 1 tablespoon of salsa over each tortilla. Sprinkle half the cheese down the center of each tortilla. Top each with half the vegetable mixture. Fold the tortilla over the ends of the filling, and then wrap it up.

Variations

1. Ham Ranch Wrap: Add 1/2 cup (125 ml) diced deli-style ham to the mixture in step 1 and substitute ranch dressing for the salsa.

2. Greek Veggie Wrap: Add 4 slices green bell pepper and 6 pitted diced kalamata olives to the mixture in step 1; omit the shredded carrot. Toss the vegetables with 2 tablespoons (30 ml) Greek dressing. Substitute 1 tablespoon (15 ml) feta cheese for the Cheddar cheese in step 3.

3. Chicken Caesar Wrap: Toss together ½ cup (125 ml) diced deli-style cooked chicken or Basic Sautéed Chicken (in this chapter), 2 cups (500 ml) shredded lettuce, 2 tablespoons (30 ml) grated Parmesan cheese, and 2 heaping tablespoon (30 ml) Caesar-style dressing for step 1. Omit the salsa and Cheddar cheese in step 3.

4. Pesto Chicken Wrap: Toss together ½ cup (125 ml) Basic Sautéed Chicken (in this chapter), 2 cups (500 ml) mixed

greens, and 2 tablespoons (30 ml) grated Asiago cheese for step 1. For step 3, substitute 1 tablespoon (15 ml) basil pesto for the salsa and omit the Cheddar cheese.

TUNA-VEGGIE MELT

Makes 2 servings

Melts are the ultimate comfort food. I made them often during my two years of travel and never tired of them. After a long morning of touring, this toasty open-face sandwich with its melted cheese hits the spot, especially if it's cold outside.

4 slices multigrain bread
4 tablespoons (60 ml) salsa
8 slices tomato
8 thin slices red onion
4 mushrooms, washed and sliced
8 slices bell pepper
2 6-ounce (170-g) cans tuna, drained
1 cup (250 ml) shredded Cheddar cheese

1. Preheat an oven or toaster oven to broil.

2. Toast the bread.

3. Spread 1 tablespoon of salsa on each piece of toast. Divide the slices of tomato, onion, mushroom, and bell pepper among the pieces of toast. Top each melt with half a can of tuna and ¼ cup (60 ml) of cheese.

4. Place the melts on a baking sheet and broil in an oven or toaster oven until the cheese is melted.

Variations

1. For extra flavor, sprinkle ¼ teaspoon (1 ml) cumin, curry powder, chili powder, thyme, oregano, or dried basil over the cheese before toasting.

2. Replace the salsa with barbecue sauce, sweet chili sauce, pesto, pizza sauce, or tomato sauce.

3. Mexi Melt: Add 5 or 6 jalapeños, chopped, and use Havarti cheese instead of the Cheddar.

4. Pizza Melt: Replace the salsa with tomato sauce left over from pasta or with pizza sauce. Substitute 4 or 5 slices of pepperoni for the tuna, and use mozzarella cheese instead of the Cheddar cheese.

CURRIED EGGS

Makes 2 servings

In New Zealand, I was invited to a potluck dinner with my coworkers. When I said I was unsure of what to bring, someone suggested I make curried eggs. "What are curried eggs?" I asked. I received a roar of laughter in response to my question. One of my workmates said, "No worries, mate. You just rock up to the party and I'll show you." I waited in suspense for days to see these famous curried eggs. It turned out to be just egg salad made with curry powder and sour cream instead of mayonnaise. That's it! But I tried it and found it was a delicious change, so I've made it this way ever since. It's tasty served on toasted whole-grain bread.

4 or 5 eggs
1 tablespoon (15 ml) salt (for boiling)

1 tablespoon (15 ml) sliced green onions
2 tablespoons (30 ml) sour cream
2 teaspoons (10 ml) mild curry powder
Salt and pepper, to taste

1. Place the eggs and the tablespoon of salt in a small saucepan and cover with at least 2 to 3 inches (5 to 7.5 cm) of water. Cover and bring to a boil over high heat.

2. When the water boils, uncover and reduce the heat to medium. Simmer for 12 minutes.

3. Using a large spoon, transfer the eggs to a bowl and run cold water over them for two to three minutes or until the eggs are cool. (If you are cooking the eggs ahead of time, store the cooled eggs in the refrigerator.)

4. Peel the cooled eggs. (I find peeling them under running water makes the task easier.) Then, over a bowl, crush the peeled eggs in your hands and crumble them into the bowl. (It's easier and faster than chopping them.)

5. Stir in the green onions, sour cream, curry powder, salt to taste, and pepper. Add more of any of these seasonings to suit your taste.

Note: Store egg salad in the refrigerator, covered; it will keep for up to one week.

Variation: For a more traditional egg salad, substitute 2 tablespoons (30 ml) light mayonnaise for the sour cream and ½ teaspoon (2 ml) Dijon-style mustard for the curry powder.

NACHOS GRANDES

Makes 2 servings

*Who doesn't like nachos? That's right—everyone
loves nachos! And nachos don't have to be unhealthy, either.
By adding beans or veggies, or both, you can bump up the
nutritional value for a better snack. Go with baked tortilla
chips if you can find them. They are generally lower in saturated
fat than are fried chips, and I find they aren't as
greasy when they're baked as nachos.*

1 15.5-ounce (439-g) can "Mexi" flavored, refried, or
    "Nacho" beans
$\frac{1}{4}$ cup (60 ml) diced tomato
$\frac{1}{4}$ cup (60 ml) diced bell pepper
$\frac{1}{4}$ cup (60 ml) diced green onion
4 large handfuls corn chips
2 cups (500 ml) shredded Cheddar cheese
$\frac{1}{4}$ cup (60 ml) salsa
$\frac{1}{4}$ cup (60 ml) light sour cream

1. In a microwavable bowl, combine the beans, tomato, pepper, and onion. Heat for one to two minutes in a microwave or until the mixture is heated through.

2. Spread the corn chips evenly over an ovensafe platter. Top with the warm bean mixture and the cheese.

3. Put the platter in an oven set to broil for about three to four minutes or until the cheese is melted.

4. Top with the salsa and light sour cream and serve immediately.

Variations

1. Before step 1, cook 8 ounces (227 g) of ground beef according to the instructions on a taco seasoning packet. Add the cooked, seasoned beef to the nachos in step 2.

2. If you can't find "Mexi" flavored or "Nacho" beans at the supermarket, substitute 1 15.5-ounce (439-g) can of baked beans mixed with 1 tablespoon (15 ml) sweet chili sauce and 1 teaspoon (5 ml) cumin.

BEAN AND VEGETABLE BURRITO

Makes 2 servings

Warning: Do not make these for your friends! They will demand you make them time and time again. With just beans, rice, and fresh vegetables, these burritos are simple, inexpensive, and healthy, too. I can't count how many times my budget was running low and I fell back on this burrito recipe. They are so delicious that you'll completely forget how good they are for you.

2 tablespoons (30 ml) vegetable oil
$\frac{1}{2}$ yellow onion, peeled and chopped
1 clove garlic, minced
$\frac{1}{2}$ green bell pepper, seeded and chopped
3 mushrooms, washed and sliced
1 15.5-ounce (439-g) can baked beans
$\frac{1}{2}$ cup (125 ml) cooked rice or Basic Rice (see Salads and Side Dishes)
1 tablespoon (15 ml) cumin, or substitute 1$\frac{1}{2}$ tablespoons (25 ml) burrito, taco, or enchilada seasoning

Salt and pepper, to taste
2 flour tortillas
2 tablespoons salsa (30 ml), divided
1 cup (250 ml) shredded Havarti cheese, divided

1. Heat the oil in a skillet over medium heat. When the oil is hot, add the onion and garlic and cook, stirring occasionally, for about one minute or until the onion is translucent.

2. Add the bell pepper and mushrooms and continue cooking and stirring for another minute or until the vegetables are tender.

3. Stir in the baked beans, cooked rice, and cumin. Continue cooking until the mixture is heated through. Season with salt and pepper and remove from heat.

4. Heat the tortillas in a microwave for 20 seconds. Spread 1 tablespoon (15 ml) salsa to one edge of each tortilla. Sprinkle half the cheese down the center of each tortilla and top with the bean and rice mixture; then fold, burrito style.

Variations

1. Beef Burrito: If you want to use beef as a protein instead of beans, just cook 8 ounces (227 g) of ground beef with taco seasoning in a frying pan until well browned, using the directions on the taco seasoning package. Substitute the beef for the beans in step 3 and proceed as directed.

2. Chicken Burrito: Prepare Basic Sautéed Chicken (in this chapter). Add the cooked chicken to the bean and rice mixture in step 3 and proceed as directed.

VEGETABLE QUESADILLA

Makes 2 quesadillas

Quesadillas are fun. They are easy to make, great to eat, and a definite crowd pleaser. When traveling, I like to make two different kinds at once and serve them with salsa, light sour cream, and a salad. Explore the variations. Create new variations. Allow yourself to be inspired by the cuisine of the place you are visiting, and you'll find that almost any fresh ingredient tastes good in a quesadilla. I especially like to try locally made pestos, salsas, and spreads for fresh, new flavors.

2 flour tortillas
3 tablespoons (45 ml) salsa
$^1\!/_2$ cup (125 ml) shredded Cheddar cheese
2 heaping tablespoons (30 ml) finely diced tomato
2 heaping tablespoons (30 ml) finely diced red onion
2 heaping tablespoons (30 ml) finely diced bell pepper
2 tablespoons (30 ml) vegetable oil

1. Spread half the salsa over each tortilla. Sprinkle 2 tablespoons (30 ml) of cheese over half of each tortilla. Top the cheese with half the tomato, onion, and pepper for each quesadilla, then sprinkle the remaining cheese over the vegetables. Fold the empty half of the tortilla over the side with the filling.

2. Lightly brush a nonstick skillet with vegetable oil and place over medium heat. When the pan is hot, gently lift a folded tortilla with a spatula and place it in the pan. Cook for two to three minutes or until golden brown. Carefully flip with a spatula and cook the other side until the tortilla is golden brown and

crispy and the cheese is melted. Remove from the pan and cut into wedges. Repeat with the other tortilla.

Variations

1. Pesto Chicken Quesadilla: Substitute 3 tablespoons (45 ml) basil pesto for the salsa. Divide ½ cup (125 ml) finely diced cooked chicken or Basic Sautéed Chicken (in this chapter) between the two tortillas. Use Parmesan cheese instead of Cheddar.

2. Barbecue Beef Quesadilla: Substitute 3 tablespoons (45 ml) barbecue sauce for the salsa. Divide ½ cup (125 ml) diced cooked beef between the two tortillas.

HUMMUS

Makes 4 cups (1 L)

My younger brother and I both worked in a restaurant in the small town of Paihia on the north island of New Zealand. It was there, and at our hostel, that we had access to a food processor. We drove every week to a neighboring town to buy chickpeas (garbanzo beans) and tahini (sesame paste) and to pick fresh lemons in order to make massive batches of hummus for our hostelling friends. We always looked forward to our chance to make our hummus again, perfecting the recipe over time. Make it in advance if you can, because it tastes best and thickens when refrigerated overnight. Tahini is readily available in most supermarkets, either with dry goods or in a cooler. I find it easier to ask a store clerk rather than searching for it. Hummus makes a great dip for veggies or pita bread.

2 15.5-ounce (439-g) cans chickpeas, drained
2 cloves garlic, peeled, crushed, and minced
1 tablespoon (15 ml) cumin
1 teaspoon (5 ml) dried coriander
3 heaping tablespoons (45 ml) tahini paste
2 tablespoons (30 ml) fresh lemon juice
⅓ cup (75 ml) olive oil
¾ cup (175 ml) water
2 to 3 dashes hot pepper sauce, such as Tabasco
1 teaspoon (5 ml) salt
1 teaspoon (5 ml) pepper

1. Place the chickpeas in the bowl of a food processor along with the garlic, cumin, coriander, tahini, and lemon juice.

2. With the food processor running, slowly pour in the oil. Then add the water little by little until the mixture is smooth and creamy. It will seem a bit runny at this point, but it will thicken in the refrigerator.

3. Season to taste with the hot pepper sauce, salt, and pepper and mix briefly.

Variations

1. Jalapeño Hummus: Add ⅓ cup (75 ml) pickled jalapeños in step 1.

2. Greek Hummus: Add 2 teaspoons (10 ml) dried basil in step 1. At the end of step 3, add ⅓ cup (75 ml) pitted and chopped kalamata olives. Mix only briefly so the olives are coarsely chopped.

TZATZIKI

Makes 2½ cups (625 ml)

Tzatziki is so cool and refreshing. It makes a delicious dip for warm pita bread, chips, or raw vegetables. You can also use it as a salad dressing or as an addition to a sandwich or wrap. One of my favorite ways to eat tzatziki is in a warm pita wrap with a generous portion of Hummus (in this chapter) and some lettuce, cucumber, and tomato. Sour cream can be used in place of yogurt, but it's not as healthy a choice. A food processor is useful for this recipe.

1 large cucumber, peeled
2 cups (500 ml) plain yogurt
1 teaspoon (5 ml) minced garlic, about 1 clove, or
    1 teaspoon (5 ml) garlic powder
2 tablespoons (30 ml) fresh lemon juice
Salt and pepper, to taste

1. Cut the cucumber in half lengthwise. Run a tablespoon down the center of the cucumber to scrape out the seeds, then cut the seeded cucumber into chunks. You should have about 2½ cups (625 ml) of chopped cucumber.

2. Place the cucumber, yogurt, garlic, and lemon juice in a food processor and puree until smooth.

3. Adjust the seasoning with salt and pepper to taste, and serve the tzatziki with warm pita bread.

Variation: In step 2, add either 1 tablespoon (15 ml) chopped fresh mint, 1 tablespoon (15 ml) chopped fresh dill, or ½ teaspoon (2 ml) chipotle paste.

EAST COAST TUNA BURGER

Makes 2 servings

If you have ever made tuna salad, you can make tuna burgers.
It's just as easy, and it is a nice change from eating cold tuna sandwiches.
This recipe allows you to get a little crazy and creative, so explore the
variations and have fun. If you prefer, substitute canned salmon for tuna.
Salmon is an excellent substitute in Variation 1, Wasabi Tuna Burger.

Tuna Patty

2 6-ounce (170-g) cans tuna, drained
$^{1}/_{2}$ cup (125 ml) bread crumbs
2 eggs
2 tablespoons (30 ml) finely chopped green onion
2 teaspoons (10 ml) lemon juice
1 teaspoon (5 ml) dried thyme
Salt and pepper, to taste
$^{1}/_{4}$ cup (60 ml) vegetable oil

Condiments

Lettuce
Tomato slices
Mustard, mayonnaise, or other favorites

Hamburger buns or rolls

1. In a bowl, combine the tuna, bread crumbs, eggs, green onion, lemon juice, thyme, salt, and pepper. If the mixture seems too runny, mix in more bread crumbs. Form the mixture into two big patties or four small patties.

2. Heat the vegetable oil in a skillet over medium-high heat. When the pan is hot, add the tuna patties and cook for three to four minutes until one side is golden brown. Flip once with a spatula and cook the other side three to four more minutes or until golden brown.

3. Serve on buns with lettuce, tomato, mustard, mayonnaise, or any favorite condiments.

Variations

1. Wasabi Tuna Burger: Omit the thyme and add 2 teaspoons (10 ml) ginger powder and 1 teaspoon (5 ml) garlic powder to the tuna mixture in step 1. Fry the patty in sesame oil instead of vegetable oil in step 2. Mix 1 teaspoon (5 ml) wasabi powder into 2 tablespoons (30 ml) mayonnaise and spread it on the burger buns as in step 3.

2. Chili Tuna Burger: Add 2 teaspoons (10 ml) chili powder, 1 teaspoon (5 ml) cumin, and 1 teaspoon (5 ml) garlic powder to the tuna mixture in step 1. Melt a piece of Cheddar cheese on the burger after you flip it in step 2. Spread 1 tablespoon (15 ml) salsa on each burger bun as in step 3.

BEEFY BURGER

Makes 6 to 8 patties

This is an instant crowd pleaser. Why buy bland supermarket burger patties when you can so easily make your own tasty blend? If you can, cook the hamburgers on a barbecue grill because it adds flavor; however, pan-frying them is fine if that's the only method available to you. And to all my traveling companions who requested (in vain) my secret burger recipe: Here you go, guys. The secret is out!

Beef Patty

1½ lbs (680 g) ground beef
1 cup (250 ml) finely diced yellow onion, about ½ large onion
1 heaping tablespoon (15 ml) minced garlic, about 2 cloves
2 teaspoons (10 ml) hot pepper sauce, such as Tabasco
¼ cup (60 ml) ketchup
2 tablespoons (30 ml) Dijon-style mustard
1 teaspoon (5 ml) salt
1 teaspoon (5 ml) pepper
3 tablespoons (45 ml) vegetable oil, divided

Condiments

Sliced tomatoes
Lettuce
Mustard, ketchup, mayonnaise, or other favorites

6 to 8 hamburger buns

1. In a large bowl, combine the ground beef with the onion, garlic, hot pepper sauce, ketchup, mustard, salt, and pepper, mixing thoroughly.

2. Shape the mixture into six to eight patties, each about ¾ inch (2 cm) thick.

3. Heat 1 tablespoon (15 ml) vegetable oil in a skillet over medium-high heat. Place two or three patties in the skillet and cook for three to four minutes, until one side is well browned. Turn once and cook until there is no pink inside the burgers and the outside is browned. Transfer the patties to a plate, add another tablespoon (15 ml) of oil to the skillet, and repeat as

needed to cook all the patties.

4. Serve the patties on burger buns with tomatoes, lettuce, and your favorite condiments.

Variations

1. Jalapeño Burger: Add ½ cup (125 ml) chopped pickled jalapeño peppers and 2 tablespoons (30 ml) taco seasoning to the beef mixture in step 1.

2. Barbecue Burger: Substitute ¼ cup (60 ml) barbecue sauce for the ketchup and add 1 tablespoon (15 ml) fresh thyme or 1 teaspoon (5ml) dried thyme to the beef mixture in step 1.

3. Mushroom Burger: Add ½ cup (125 ml) finely diced mushrooms to the beef mixture in step 1.

VEGETARIAN BURGER

Makes 5 patties

I first found this recipe when I was working in a vegetarian restaurant in Australia. I wrote it down and then forgot all about it. Later in my travels, my roommate and I were peering into our refrigerator one day, pondering what we could do with all the leftover rice we had. I checked through some recipes and found this one. After a few modifications, I found the perfect solution for leftover rice; you can also use Basic Rice (see Salads and Side Dishes).

Patty

2 cups (500 ml) cooked rice

½ cup (125 ml) shredded zucchini, about ½ zucchini

½ cup (125 ml) shredded carrot, about 1 carrot

½ cup (125 ml) finely diced yellow onion, about ½ onion

½ cup (125 ml) finely diced celery, about 1 celery stalk

½ cup (125 ml) finely diced bell pepper, about ½ pepper

1 tablespoon (15 ml) crushed and minced garlic, about 1
    clove, or 1 teaspoon (5 ml) garlic powder

1 cup (250 ml) all-purpose flour

¼ cup (60 ml) sweet chili sauce

½ teaspoon (2 ml) cumin

½ teaspoon (2 ml) dried coriander

½ tablespoon (7 ml) salt

1 teaspoon (5 ml) pepper

¼ cup (60 ml) vegetable oil, divided

Condiments

Lettuce

Tomato slices

Mustard, mayonnaise, or your favorites

5 burger buns or rolls

1. Allow the cooked rice to drain in a colander until cool enough to handle, or warm leftover rice in a microwave. See Note.

2. In a bowl, mix the rice with the zucchini, carrot, onion, celery, bell pepper, garlic, flour, sweet chili sauce, cumin, coriander, salt, and pepper until the mixture has a sticky consistency. Shape into five patties, each about ½ inch (1 cm) thick.

3. Heat 2 tablespoons of the vegetable oil in a large non-stick skillet over high heat. Place two or three patties in the skillet and cook for two to three minutes. Don't try to flip them too quickly or they will stick and fall apart. When the first side is

golden brown, gently slide a spatula under each patty and flip it over. Continue cooking for another two to three minutes until golden brown. Transfer the cooked patties to a plate, add the remaining 2 tablespoons of vegetable oil to the skillet, and repeat with the second batch of patties.

4. Serve the patties on burger buns with lettuce, tomatoes, and your favorite condiments.

Note: To heat leftover rice, add 2 tablespoons (30 ml) of water to a bowl of rice. Cover and heat in a microwave on High for two to three minutes or until the rice is warm and sticky.

Variation: Omit the sweet chili sauce and substitute 1 egg and 1 tablespoon (15 ml) curry powder in step 2.

BARBECUE STEAK SANDWICH

Makes 2 sandwiches

I love this sandwich. It always satisfies my barbecue cravings when I'm traveling. I like to add a couple slices of Cheddar cheese at the end, then melt it in a toaster oven. For a more "carb conscious" sandwich, substitute a tortilla wrap or pita for the bread. You can also transform it into a great dinner by serving the steak mixture over Garlic Smashed Potatoes (see Salads and Side Dishes). Once, for my big Australian friend Glen, I made this using both beef and chicken in one sandwich. I can still hear his Aussie voice saying, "Moike! This is a great sandwich, mate!"

2 tablespoons (30 ml) vegetable oil
8 ounces (227 g) rib-eye steak or stir-fry beef
Salt and pepper, to taste

8 to 10 slices peeled yellow onion

2 small cloves garlic, peeled and minced

$\frac{1}{4}$ cup (60 ml) diced bell pepper

2 large mushrooms, washed and sliced

$\frac{1}{4}$ cup (60 ml) barbecue sauce

2 to 3 drops hot pepper sauce, such as Tabasco

4 slices whole-grain bread, toasted

1. Heat the oil in a small skillet over medium heat. While the pan is heating, cut the steak into thin strips and season with salt and pepper.

2. When the skillet is hot, add the onion and garlic. Cook, stirring occasionally, for about one minute or until the onion is translucent. Add the pepper and mushrooms and cook, stirring occasionally, for another minute or until the vegetables start to soften.

3. Add the steak to the skillet and cook, stirring frequently, until the steak is lightly browned. Stir in the barbecue sauce and the hot pepper sauce and bring to a simmer. If you like the steak medium, remove the skillet from the heat. If you prefer the steak well done, cook for an additional minute or two.

4. Transfer the steak mixture to the toasted bread and serve immediately.

Variation

Barbecue Chicken Sandwich: Replace the beef with one large chicken breast thinly sliced. Proceed as directed, making sure the chicken is thoroughly cooked in step 3.

Salads and Side Dishes

BEAN MEDLEY SALAD

Makes 2 servings

*This salad originates from one of my more unusual jobs.
I worked at a mine in Australia's Northern Territory, and one of my
many responsibilities was to prepare a cold salad bar for the miners.
One of the bulk ingredients they ordered in was a canned "six bean
medley." So I whipped up a Thai version of the beans with some fresh
veggies (see Variation 1, below). Because it was my first time cooking
for Australian miners, I was a bit nervous about how they would
respond to this healthy fare. But it got rave reviews from the miners,
and from that day forward, they wolfed it down on a daily basis.
If it passed the hungry miner test, you know it must be good!*

2 15-ounce (425-g) cans mixed beans
$^1\!/_2$ cup (125 ml) finely diced green bell pepper
$^1\!/_2$ cup (125 ml) finely diced tomato
$^1\!/_2$ cup (125 ml) finely diced red onion
$^1\!/_3$ cup (75 ml) wine vinegar, balsamic vinegar, or cider
  vinegar
3 tablespoons (45 ml) olive oil
1 tablespoon (15 ml) granulated sugar, honey, or artificial
  sweetener
2 teaspoons (10 ml) dried basil
$^1\!/_2$ teaspoon (2 ml) hot pepper sauce
Salt and pepper, to taste

Mix all the ingredients together in a bowl and serve. Or
refrigerate overnight to better blend the flavors.

Note: If you can't find cans of mixed beans, just select one can each of two different kinds of beans. You can use baby lima beans, black-eyed peas, garbanzo beans, white or red kidney beans, or romano beans.

Variations

1. Thai Bean Salad. Omit the vinegar, olive oil, sugar, basil, and hot pepper sauce. Add 3 tablespoons (45 ml) sweet chili sauce, 1 teaspoon (5 ml) cumin, and 1 teaspoon (5 ml) coriander.

2. Greek Bean Salad. Omit the vinegar, sugar, and hot pepper sauce. Increase the olive oil to ¼ cup (60 ml), and add 2 tablespoons (30 ml) lemon juice, ¼ cup (60 ml) pitted kalamata olives, ½ teaspoon (2 ml) dried oregano, and ½ teaspoon (2 ml) dried basil.

SUMMER FRESH TOMATO–BASIL SALAD

Makes 2 servings

This summer salad is the perfect excuse to visit an open-air market. Because it is such a simple and delicate recipe, using the finest ingredients is very important. Select vine-ripened organic tomatoes, if possible. They are more expensive, but they have much more flavor than regular grocery-store tomatoes. Choose a nice, dark-colored extra-virgin olive oil. In most supermarkets, you can find smaller 16-ounce (500-ml) bottles that won't break your budget. Serve this salad with good crusty bread for a light lunch or as a side dish for dinner.

3 roma or small tomatoes, cut into bite-size pieces—about 1 to 1½ cups (250 to 375 ml)
3 to 4 fresh basil leaves, sliced in thin strips

3 tablespoons (45 ml) extra virgin olive oil
Salt and pepper, to taste

Gently combine all the ingredients in a bowl and serve.

Variations

1. Mix in 2 tablespoons (30 ml) crumbled goat cheese.
2. Mix in ¼ cup (60 ml) thinly sliced red onion.
3. Mix in ½ cup (125 ml) diced bell pepper and 5 to 10 kalamata olives.

PASTA SALAD

Makes 4 servings

*I consider this to be another "market-friendly" recipe.
Use the freshest vegetables you can find at the local market to fully
enjoy the flavors. Even if you are traveling alone, go ahead and
prepare the full recipe. This salad keeps well in the refrigerator for up
to a week, making lunches a snap. It's also great for a light summer
dinner or as a side dish. For a heartier salad, add Basic Sautéed
Chicken (see Sandwiches, Wraps, and Snacks).*

2 cups (500 ml) uncooked penne, bow tie, spiral, or
   similar pasta
¼ cup (60 ml) peeled and sliced red onion
¼ cup (60 ml) grated carrot
⅓ cup (75 ml) seeded and sliced bell pepper
10 small broccoli florets
½ cup (125 ml) Italian dressing
Salt and pepper, to taste

Continued on page 65

Below: Backpacker's Muesli

Below: Pancakes
Right: Spinach and Tomato Frittata

Left: French Toast
Below: Vegetable Quesadilla

Left: Veggie Wrap

Below: Hummus

Below: Beefy Burger
Right: Darwin Salad

Below: Asian Beef Salad
Left: Pizza

Below: Pasta Bolognese
Right: Mixed Vegetable Stir-Fry

Below: Barbecue Steak Sandwich
Right: Strawberry Crêpe

Below: Nachos Grandes

Continued from page 48

1. Place a large pot of water, with a dash of salt added, over high heat. Cover and bring to a boil.

2. Add the pasta and reduce the heat to medium-high. Simmer uncovered, stirring occasionally, for about 10 minutes or until the pasta is tender but firm.

3. Drain the pasta in a colander, then run cold water over it until it is completely cooled. Allow the pasta to drain thoroughly.

4. Transfer the pasta to a large bowl and add the onion, carrot, pepper, and broccoli. Toss with the dressing and season with salt and pepper.

Note: If you prefer the broccoli slightly cooked, add the florets to the boiling water and pasta about one minute before you drain the pasta.

Variations

1. Creamy Pasta Salad: Replace the Italian dressing with ⅓ cup (75 ml) light mayonnaise, 1 teaspoon (5 ml) prepared mustard, and a dash of hot sauce.

2. Creamy Barbecue Pasta Salad. Replace the Italian dressing with ⅓ cup (75 ml) light mayonnaise and 2 teaspoons (10 ml) barbecue sauce. Add ½ cup (125 ml) thinly sliced and chopped deli roast beef with the vegetables in step 4.

POTATO SALAD

Makes 4 to 5 servings

No matter where you are, a summer picnic just is not complete without a nice, chilled potato salad. As for Hash Browns (see Breakfast), the boiled potatoes must cool for at least two hours before you

*dice them, so it's easiest to cook them a day ahead. I like larger
recipes like this one because I can make the salad for lunch
and save the leftover salad in the refrigerator
for a quick snack anytime.*

4 or 5 large baking potatoes, washed
$^{1}/_{2}$ tablespoon (7.5 ml) salt
$^{1}/_{2}$ cup (125 ml) diced green onion
$^{1}/_{2}$ cup (125 ml) light mayonnaise
1 tablespoon (15 ml) Dijon-style mustard
Salt and pepper, to taste

1. Place the potatoes and salt in a large pot and add water until the potatoes are covered by at least 3 inches of water. Cover and bring to a boil over high heat. Reduce the heat to medium-low and simmer for about 15 to 20 minutes. After the first 10 minutes, check the potatoes for doneness every couple of minutes. The potatoes are done when easily pierced with a fork.

2. Remove the pot from the heat, drain the water from the pan, and allow the potatoes to cool. Do not run cold water over them because that will make them soggy. When the potatoes are no longer steaming, place them uncovered in the refrigerator and cool them completely. (This may take up to two hours.)

3. Cut the cooled potatoes into $^{1}/_{2}$-inch (1 cm) bite-size pieces. You'll have about 4 to 6 cups (1 to 1.5 L) of chopped potatoes. In a large bowl, gently combine the potatoes, onions, mayonnaise, mustard, salt, and pepper.

Note: Cover and refrigerate leftovers, which will keep for up to one week.

Variations

1. Add 10 green olives, chopped, and ½ cup (125 ml) chopped sun-dried tomatoes.

2. Add ½ cup (125 ml) diced celery, ½ cup (125 ml) diced bell pepper, and 5 boiled eggs, chopped. (To boil eggs, see Curried Eggs, in Sandwiches, Wraps, and Snacks.)

3. Add 1 cup (250 ml) diced chicken or Basic Sautéed Chicken (see Sandwiches, Wraps, and Snacks) and substitute ½ cup (125 ml) prepared Caesar dressing for the mustard and mayonnaise.

TACO SALAD

Makes 2 servings

Whoever invented the taco salad was a genius. It tastes a bit sinful, but it is actually a nutritious, healthy meal. It's also nice and light, so you'll have the energy to go tango dancing after dinner! To add some crunch, toss a handful of crushed corn chips into the salad mix.

2 cups (500 ml) shredded leaf lettuce

1 large tomato, diced

½ avocado, peeled and diced

½ cup (125 ml) seeded and diced red bell pepper

2 tablespoons (30 ml) chopped green onion

1/4 cup (60 ml) salsa or taco sauce

2 tablespoons (30 ml) light sour cream

10 to 12 fresh jalapeño peppers, seeded and chopped (optional)

½ cup (125ml) shredded Cheddar, Havarti, or Colby cheese

1. In a bowl, mix together the lettuce, tomato, avocado, bell pepper, and green onion.

2. Divide the lettuce mixture between two plates and top each with half the salsa, sour cream, jalapeño peppers, and cheese.

Variations

1. For zesty sour cream, add a squeeze of lime or lemon juice and 1 tablespoon (15 ml) taco seasoning to the 2 tablespoons (30 ml) of sour cream.

2. Beef Taco Salad: Prepare ½ pound (227 g) of ground beef according to the directions on a taco seasoning packet. Allow the cooked beef to cool slightly, then add it to the salad in step 2.

3. Chicken Taco Salad: Prepare ½ pound (227 g) of ground chicken according to the directions on a taco seasoning packet. Make sure the chicken is thoroughly cooked, with no pink visible in the center, then add it to the salad in step 2.

4. Bean Taco Salad: Drain and add 1 cup (250 ml) canned pinto beans to the lettuce mixture in step 1.

DARWIN SALAD

Makes 2 servings

I created this salad in Darwin, Australia, where it's hot—really hot—and you don't want to eat any heavy meals. I needed something light but also with some protein. Baked beans on a salad? I know it sounds odd, but try it! I made this salad many times for my Australian friends, and they loved it. I'm sure you will, too.

4 cups (1L) mixed leaf lettuce
1 medium-size tomato, diced

8 slices red onion
8 slices bell pepper
$1/2$ cup (125 ml) shredded carrot
$1/4$ cup (60 ml) canned baked beans
$1/4$ cup (60 ml) sweet chili sauce
1 6-ounce (170-g) can tuna, drained
1 avocado, peeled and diced
$1/2$ cup (125 ml) alfalfa sprouts
$1/2$ cup (125 ml) shredded Cheddar cheese

1. Place the lettuce, tomato, onion, bell pepper, and carrot in a bowl.

2. Add the baked beans and sweet chili sauce, mixing gently until the salad is coated with the sauce. Divide the mixture between two plates.

3. Top each salad with half the tuna, avocado, sprouts, and cheese.

Variation: Substitute 2 tablespoons (30 ml) salsa for the sweet chili sauce.

ASIAN BEEF SALAD

Makes 2 servings

Even though this recipe calls for presliced stir-fry beef, I prefer to use rib-eye steak for this salad. It takes a few minutes of preparation and is a bit more expensive, but it tastes better. If you have time, marinate the beef in the garlic, ginger, and sweet chili sauce for a couple of hours. This beef preparation is also terrific in a wrap for lunch or a picnic.

Beef

1/2 lb (227 g) thinly sliced stir-fry beef

2 teaspoons (10 ml) minced garlic, about 2 cloves

2 teaspoons (10 ml) peeled and minced fresh ginger

4 tablespoons (60 ml) sweet chili sauce, divided

2 tablespoons (30 ml) sesame oil, or any oil if you don't
have sesame oil

Salt and pepper, to taste

Salad

4 cups (1 L) mixed Asian greens, or any blend of baby
spinach, mizuna, red and green chard, red mustard
greens, arugula, or tatsoi greens

1 tomato, sliced into wedges

1/4 cup (60 ml) finely diced green onions

1/2 cup (125 ml) bean sprouts

Dressing

2 tablespoons (30 ml) sesame oil

1/4 cup (60 ml) rice wine vinegar

2 tablespoons (30 ml) sweet chili sauce

1 heaping tablespoon (15 ml) finely chopped fresh cilantro

1. To prepare the beef, combine it in a bowl with the garlic,
ginger, and 2 tablespoons (30 ml) of the sweet chili sauce.

2. Heat the 2 tablespoons of sesame oil in a skillet over
medium-high heat. When the oil is hot, add the beef mixture
and cook, stirring frequently, until the beef is lightly browned.

3. Add the remaining 2 tablespoons (30 ml) of sweet chili

sauce, stirring to coat the beef. Continue cooking for about two to three minutes or until the beef is no longer pink in the middle. Remove from heat and season with salt and pepper.

4. Gently toss all the salad ingredients together in a bowl.

5. Prepare the dressing by vigorously mixing all the ingredients together in a small bowl with a fork or a whisk. Toss the salad with the dressing and divide the salad between two plates. Top each salad with half the beef and serve.

Variations

1. Substitute black bean sauce, sweet-and-sour sauce, teriyaki sauce, or any bottled stir-fry sauce for the sweet chili sauce.

2. Substitute ½ pound (227 g) sliced chicken or tofu for the beef and proceed as directed.

3. Add 2 ounces (63g) of cooked rice noodles to the salad in step 4 and continue with the recipe as directed.

BASIC RICE

Makes 2 servings

I know instant rice seems like the easiest way to go, but it falls far short of the nutritional value of brown rice. In this method, whether you use brown or white rice, you cook it just as you would cook pasta, so it's a snap. Though the common standard is ½ cup (125 ml) of uncooked rice per serving, I can't be bothered to make such a small amount, so I use 1 cup (250 ml) of uncooked rice and make two servings.

1 cup (250 ml) uncooked long-grain brown or white rice
1 teaspoon (5 ml) salt
6 cups (1.5 L) water

1. If you are using brown rice, rinse it thoroughly in a colander and drain.

2. Place the rice, salt, and water in a large saucepan. Cover and bring to a boil over high heat, stirring occasionally.

3. Reduce the heat to medium-low, remove the lid, and simmer, stirring occasionally. If you are using white rice, simmer for 15 to 20 minutes. If you are using brown rice, simmer for 35 to 40 minutes. The rice is done when it is soft to the bite but still just a bit firm.

4. Drain the rice in a colander as you would for pasta. If you are making the rice ahead for another day, run cold water over it for one minute and store, covered, in the refrigerator for up to one week. Or serve it immediately with Mixed Vegetable Stir-Fry or Green Curry Stir-Fry (see Dinner).

Variation

Flavored Rice: Stir in the contents of a seasoning packet from any flavor of ramen ("two-minute") noodles to the rice after it is cooked and drained. That adds great flavor to almost any rice dish.

GARLIC SMASHED POTATOES

Makes 2 servings

Have you ever had fabulous mashed potatoes and wondered why they tasted so good? The secret is seasoning them well with salt and pepper. That's the key to making regular mashed potatoes into stellar mashed potatoes. After you have completed step 5 in this recipe, taste the potatoes. If you think they need a bit more seasoning,

*add additional salt and/or pepper in ½-teaspoon (2-ml)
increments; this prevents overseasoning. Mix, then taste again.
After a couple of adjustments, you'll notice the difference.*

2 large baking potatoes, washed—and peeled, if desired
1 tablespoon (15 ml) salt
2 tablespoons (30 ml) butter
2 tablespoons (30 ml) milk
1 small clove garlic, minced, or 1 teaspoon (5 ml) garlic
   powder
Salt and pepper, to taste

1. Chop the potatoes into chunks; the smaller the chunks, the faster they will cook.

2. Place the potatoes and salt in a pot and add water until the potatoes are covered by about 3 inches. Bring to a boil over high heat.

3. Reduce heat to medium and simmer for 12 to 15 minutes or until the potatoes can be easily pierced with a fork.

4. Drain the potatoes in a colander, then transfer them back into the pot.

5. Add the butter, milk, garlic, salt, and pepper. Smash the potatoes using a potato masher or a fork. Serve warm.

Variations

Add any of the following in step 5:

1 teaspoon (5 ml) wasabi; this complements a fish dish
   nicely

1½ tablespoons (20 ml) blue cheese; this complements
   steak and other meat dishes

2 tablespoons (30 ml) mixed herbs—any combination of
dried rosemary, thyme, basil, oregano, or tarragon

1 tablespoon (15 ml) curry powder

1 tablespoon (15 ml) chili powder

½ cup (125 ml) frozen mixed vegetables, thawed, in
combination with any of the above

WILD WILD RICE

Makes 2 to 3 servings

Wild rice is one of the most nutritious kinds of rice. Some
people avoid cooking with it because it looks so different, but the
trick to preparing it is to cook it as you would cook pasta. Use at
least three to four times the amount of water to rice. That's it!
If you have cooked pasta before, you can make wild rice.

1 tablespoon (15 ml) salt

1 cup (250 ml) raw uncooked wild rice, well rinsed in a
colander

½ cup (125 ml) grated carrot

¼ cup (60 ml) chopped green onion, white and green parts

1 tablespoon (15 ml) dried ginger powder

1 teaspoon (5 ml) garlic powder

1 tablespoon (15 ml) honey (optional)

Salt and pepper, to taste

1. Fill a saucepan three-quarters full with water. Add the
salt and bring to a boil over high heat.

2. Add the rice and bring back to a boil. Then reduce the

heat and simmer, uncovered, for 20 to 30 minutes. When the rice splits open and is soft to the bite, drain it in a colander.

3. Transfer the rice back to the saucepan and stir in the carrot, green onion, ginger powder, garlic powder, and honey (if using). Season with salt and pepper, and serve.

Variations

1. Berry Wild Rice: Add ½ cup (125 ml) dried cranberries or dried blueberries to the cooked rice at the end of step 2, 30 seconds before draining it. You can also try dried cherries or chopped dried apricots. You'll be surprised how well these flavors go with wild rice.

2. Easiest Wild Wild Rice: Substitute 1 cup (250 ml) frozen vegetables, thawed, for the fresh carrots and green onions. Eliminate the dried ginger and honey and adjust the garlic powder to 1 tablespoon (15 ml). Add 1 tablespoon (15 ml) onion powder. Stir in the frozen vegetables, garlic powder, and onion powder with the cooked rice as in step 3, and season with salt and pepper.

3. Wild Rice Pancakes: For a quick side dish, add ¾ cup (175 ml) cooked, unseasoned wild rice, as at the end of step 2, to the batter for Pancakes (see Breakfast) and cook the pancakes as directed.

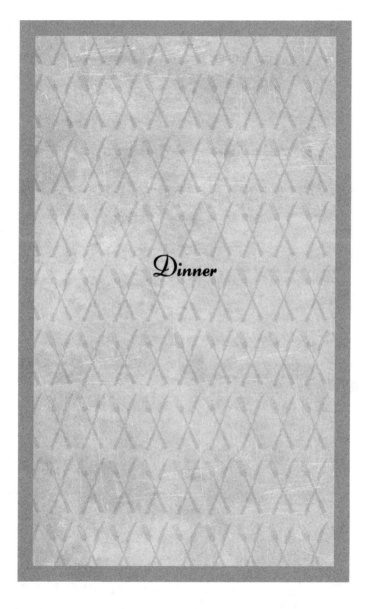

Dinner

ASIAN VEGGIE NOODLE BOWL

Makes 1 serving

If you are a backpacker, I know at some point in your travels you've probably bought some ramen, or "two-minute," noodles. Here's a way to make them a bit healthier and a lot more flavorful. You can use almost any combination of vegetables. Just make sure you chop them fairly small so they cook as fast as the noodles. Once I discovered garlic–chili paste (a Thai condiment known as sambal oelek*), it became my personal favorite. But watch out: garlic–chili pastes can be quite spicy. You can easily substitute hoisin sauce, spicy Szechuan sauce, or black bean paste for different flavors.*

1 package ramen noodles, Oriental flavor
6 to 8 small broccoli florets
1 green onion, sliced
2 mushrooms, washed and sliced
1 teaspoon (5 ml) garlic–chili paste

1. Place the noodles and the contents of the flavor packet included in the package into a small saucepan along with the broccoli, onion, and mushrooms. Add enough water to just cover the noodles and vegetables.

2. Bring to a boil over high heat and cook for about two minutes or until the noodles are soft. Remove from heat and cool for one minute.

3. Drain off the liquid until there is about 1 inch (3 cm) of liquid remaining in the pan. Stir in the garlic–chili paste, transfer the soup to a bowl, and serve immediately.

Variation: Top off the finished soup by adding 6 ounces

(170 g) of tofu, diced cooked chicken or Basic Sautéed Chicken (see Sandwiches, Wraps, and Snacks), or cooked beef from the Asian Beef Salad (see Salads and Side Dishes).

PAN-FRIED FISH

Makes 2 servings

When I was in Gove, northern Australia, I was lucky enough to work with a chef who was also a fisherman. We went ocean fishing one day and caught a huge fish he told me was called a threadfin salmon. It looked nothing like the salmon I was accustomed to in North America. After he cleaned it, he gave me a couple of salmon steaks to take home. I wanted to get the full flavor, so I just sautéed the fish in plain butter with a little garlic. Wow, was I impressed. It tasted just like sautéed prawns! No matter what the local fish specialty is, you'll find that this simple preparation brings out its delicate flavors. Serve with potatoes and a simple green salad for a satisfying meal.

½ cup (125 ml) canola oil, divided
2 6- to 8-ounce (170- to 227-g) fish steaks or fillets
1 tablepoon (15 ml) lemon pepper, divided
Salt, to taste

1. Heat 3 to 4 tablespoons (45 ml to 60 ml) of the oil in a large skillet over medium-high heat.

2. Season the fish with 1½ teaspoons (7 ml) lemon pepper, and add salt to taste. When the skillet is hot, place the fish in the pan and reduce the heat to medium. Cook for three to four min-

utes or until the first side is golden brown. Turn the fillet and cook for another three minutes or until the fish flakes easily when tested with a fork. Repeat with second fillet.

Note: A 6- to 8-ounce (170- to 227-g) portion of fish will take about three to four minutes per side. A 10- to 12-ounce (283- to 340-g) portion of fish will take four to six minutes per side.

Variations

Replace the lemon pepper with any of the following:

1 tablespoon (15 ml) Italian herb mix

1 teaspoon (5 ml) each of dried oregano, basil, thyme, and parsley

1 tablespoon (15 ml) Mexican spice mix

1 teaspoon (5 ml) each of ground cumin, garlic powder, and onion powder, plus a tiny pinch of cayenne

BACKPACKER CHILI

Makes 2 servings

This is one of the easiest and least-expensive recipes in this book to prepare. I can't count the number of times I have made this after a day of snowboarding in Queenstown, New Zealand. It's perfect for the evenings when you are really tired and just need something fast but still healthy. This chili is great served with garlic toast.

2 tablespoons (30 ml) vegetable oil

2 heaping tablespoons (30 ml) diced yellow onion

2 cloves garlic, peeled and minced

8 mushrooms, washed and chopped

2 heaping tablespoons (30 ml) chopped bell pepper

2 15-ounce (425-g) cans baked beans

2 tablespoons (30 ml) chili powder

¼ cup (60 ml) sweet chili sauce (optional), or increase chili
   powder to 2 teaspoons (10 ml)

Salt and pepper, to taste

½ cup (125 ml) shredded Cheddar cheese (optional)

1. Heat the oil in a skillet over medium-high heat. When the oil is hot, add the onion and garlic and cook, stirring occasionally, for one to two minutes or until the onion is translucent.

2. Add the mushrooms and bell pepper and continue cooking and stirring for another minute or until the vegetables are tender.

3. Stir in the baked beans, chili powder, and sweet chili sauce (if using) and cook until the mixture is thoroughly heated. Season with salt and pepper. Divide the chili between two bowls and top each bowl with ¼ cup (60 ml) grated cheese.

Variation: At the end of step 1, add ½ pound (227 g) of minced beef or chicken to the onion and garlic mixture. Cook, stirring occasionally, until the meat is tender and no longer pink in the middle. Continue as directed.

HEARTY CHILI

Makes 5 to 6 servings

*This chili takes more time to prepare than
most of my other recipes do, but it's an inexpensive
way to feed several people. The longer you simmer it, the
better it will taste. If you don't have time
to simmer it for at least a half hour, omit the
beef stock, water, or beer. Serve with a
side of garlic toast.*

2 tablespoons (30 ml) vegetable oil

4 strips uncooked bacon, diced, or ½ cup (125 ml)
    uncooked lean ground bacon

1 small yellow onion, diced, about 6 heaping tablespoons
    (90 ml)

2 cloves garlic, peeled and minced

1 pound (454 g) lean ground beef

10 mushrooms, washed and sliced

1 ancho chile pepper, diced

1 red bell pepper, diced

1 28-ounce (794-g) can diced tomatoes

1 15-ounce (425-g) can kidney beans, drained

½ cup (125 ml) beef stock, water, or beer

1 5.5-ounce (156-ml) can tomato paste

2 tablespoons (30 ml) fresh lime juice

¼ cup (60 ml) mild chili powder

½ teaspoon (2 ml) hot pepper sauce

1 tablespoon (15 ml) salt

1 tablespoon (15 ml) pepper

1. Heat the oil in a large pot over medium heat. When the oil is hot, add the bacon, onion, and garlic and cook, stirring, for two to three minutes or until the onion is translucent.

2. Add the beef, mushrooms, ancho chile, and bell pepper. Increase the heat to medium-high and cook, stirring occasionally, until the beef is browned.

3. Add the diced tomatoes, kidney beans, beef stock, tomato paste, lime juice, chili powder, hot pepper sauce, salt, and pepper and bring to a boil.

4. Reduce the heat to low and simmer for 30 minutes, stirring occasionally.

Variations

1. Substitute minced chicken or minced pork for the ground beef and proceed as directed.

2. Sloppy Joes: Serve the chili on toasted hamburger buns topped with grated Cheddar cheese and diced raw onions.

VEGETABLE FRIED RICE

Makes 2 servings

Do you have leftover rice and vegetables in your refrigerator? Fried rice is another one of those meals that I have made time and time again, everywhere I have traveled. It's a very flavorful and beautiful dish if you get the first steps right. The first key is to use sesame oil. The next key is to sauté the onion, garlic, and gingerroot without browning them. Once you've done this, you're guaranteed a good base flavor. Always use cold or chilled rice when making fried rice, because warm rice tends to stick to the pan. Adding some cooked beef or chicken to the finished rice transforms it into a complete and nutritious meal.

3 tablespoons (45 ml) sesame or canola oil

$^1/_4$ cup (60 ml) finely diced yellow onion

1 teaspoon (5 ml) crushed or minced garlic

1 teaspoon (5 ml) grated or minced fresh gingerroot

$^1/_4$ cup (60 ml) diced carrot

$^1/_4$ cup (60 ml) diced bell pepper

$^1/_4$ cup (60 ml) sliced mushrooms

$^1/_4$ cup (60 ml) sliced snow peas

2 cups (500 ml) cooked rice, or Basic Rice (see Salads and Side Dishes)

1 to 2 tablespoons (15 ml to 30 ml) soy sauce

Salt and pepper, to taste

1. Heat the oil in a skillet over medium-high to high heat. When the oil is hot, add the onion, garlic, and ginger and cook, stirring occasionally, for about one minute or until the onion is translucent.

2. Stir in the carrot, bell pepper, mushrooms, and snow peas and cook, stirring, for another two to three minutes or until the vegetables are tender.

3. Reduce the heat to medium. Add the cooked rice and cook for three to four more minutes, adding the soy sauce little by little and stirring constantly until the rice is heated through and has a golden brown color. Season with salt and pepper, and serve.

Note: To make an even simpler fried rice, use mixed frozen vegetables in place of the fresh veggies.

Variation: Before step 1, whisk 2 eggs together in a cup with a fork. Then heat 1 tablespoon (15 ml) canola or sesame oil in a skillet over high heat. When the oil is hot, pour the egg mixture into the skillet, tilting the pan so the mix spreads out and cooks through. (Do not stir.) Remove the flat egg from the pan with a spatula. Slice it into thin strips and set aside. Proceed with the recipe as directed, then top the finished rice with the sliced egg before serving.

MIXED VEGETABLE STIR-FRY

Makes 2 servings

I've seen a lot of backpackers prepare stir-fries. I've also noticed that most of those dishes lacked any excitement. One of the secrets to good flavor is to always begin by sautéing the onions, garlic, and gingerroot in sesame or canola oil, unless you are adding a curry spice. If you plan to add curry, you should begin with vegetable oil so the flavors don't compete. Once you master the basic technique, you'll find you can create an almost endless number of flavorful combinations using different vegetables, curries, sauces, and pastes.

2 tablespoons (30 ml) sesame, canola, or vegetable oil
½ cup (125 ml) diced yellow onion
2 small cloves of garlic, peeled, crushed, and minced
2 teaspoons (10 ml) grated or minced fresh gingerroot
2 chicken breasts, diced, about 1 cup (250 ml)
2 cups (500 ml) of mixed sliced vegetables such as carrot,
    bell pepper, zucchini, and Chinese cabbage
1 cup (250 ml) sweet-and-sour sauce
Salt and pepper, to taste
2 cups (500 ml) cooked rice or Basic Rice (see Salads and
    Side Dishes)

1. Heat the oil in a skillet over medium heat. When the oil is hot, add the onion, garlic, and gingerroot and cook, stirring constantly, for about one minute or until the onion is translucent.

2. Add the diced chicken and mixed vegetables and continue cooking and stirring for two to three minutes or until the vegetables are tender and the chicken is no longer pink on the outside.

3. Stir in the sweet-and-sour sauce, bring to a simmer, and continue cooking for about two to three minutes or until the sauce thickens and the chicken is no longer pink in the middle. Season to taste with salt and pepper and serve over the cooked rice.

Variations

1. Substitute hoisin, teriyaki, or black bean sauce for the sweet-and-sour sauce.

2. Substitute 1 cup (250 ml) diced tofu, pork, or beef for the chicken.

3. Substitute ramen ("two-minute") noodles for the rice. Prepare the noodles with the flavor packet according to the package directions. Drain off all the liquid before topping the noodles with the stir-fry.

GREEN CURRY STIR-FRY

Makes 2 servings

If you have never made a green curry before, prepare to fall in love. This recipe has texture and flavor that are quite different from those of the Mixed Vegetable Stir-Fry (in this chapter). The curry adds a spicy, robust bite, which is balanced by the creamy, sweet coconut milk. Green curry pastes can vary in potency depending on the brand you use. After you have made this recipe once, you may want to adjust the amount. You can also replace the green curry paste with red, yellow, Panang, or Massaman curry paste. If you can't find coconut milk, use whipping cream or half-and-half instead.

1 tablespoon (15 ml) vegetable oil
2 tablespoons (30 ml) diced yellow onion
1 clove of garlic, crushed and minced
1 tablespoon (15 ml) green curry paste
½ cup (125 ml) sliced Chinese cabbage
½ cup (125 ml) sliced eggplant
6 mushrooms, washed and sliced
½ carrot, thinly sliced
1 large chicken breast, diced, or 6 ounces (170 g) tofu, diced
2 cups (500 ml) coconut milk
Salt and pepper, to taste
2 cups (500 ml) cooked rice or Basic Rice (see Salads and Side Dishes)

1. Heat the vegetable oil in a skillet over medium heat. When the oil is hot, add the onion, garlic, and green curry paste and cook for one minute or until the onion is translucent.

2. Add the cabbage, eggplant, mushrooms, carrot, and chicken or tofu. Cook, stirring occasionally, for two to three minutes or until the vegetables are tender and the chicken is no longer pink on the outside.

3. Stir in the coconut milk and continue cooking for another two minutes or until the chicken is cooked through and the sauce thickens. Season to taste with salt and pepper, and serve over the cooked rice.

SATAY CHICKEN STIR-FRY

Makes 2 servings

*Most of the people I have met while traveling
remember me for this recipe. Friends from Brisbane,
Australia, to New Jersey love this spicy peanut stir-fry.
Inspired by the Thai noodle dish known as Pad Thai, this recipe
takes ramen noodles to a whole new level. With some chicken and
fresh vegetables and just a few minutes of effort, you can
transform those bland noodles into a tasty and nutritionally
complete meal. For a vegetarian version, simply
substitute diced extra-firm tofu for the chicken.*

2 3-ounce (85-g) packages ramen noodles, chicken or
    vegetable flavor, prepared according to package directions
2 tablespoons (30 ml) canola or sesame oil
¼ cup (60 ml) diced yellow onion
2 cloves of garlic, peeled and crushed or minced
1 teaspoon (5 ml) peeled and minced or grated fresh
    gingerroot
1 teaspoon (5 ml) dried red pepper flakes (optional)
2 chicken breasts, diced, or 12 ounces (340 g) tofu, diced
¼ cup (60 ml) peeled sliced carrot
¼ cup (60 ml) sliced bell pepper
¼ cup (60 ml) sliced zucchini
3 tablespoons (45 ml) smooth peanut butter
1 tablespoon (15 ml) sweet chili sauce
Salt and pepper, to taste

1. Drain the flavored broth from the prepared noodles,

reserving ¼ cup (175 ml) of the broth. Set the noodles and reserved broth aside in separate bowls.

2. Heat the oil in a skillet over medium heat. When the oil is hot, add the onion, garlic, gingerroot, and red pepper flakes (if using) and cook, stirring occasionally, for about one to two minutes or until the onion is translucent.

3. Add the chicken or tofu, carrot, bell pepper, and zucchini. Continue cooking, stirring occasionally, for another one to two minutes or until the vegetables are tender.

4. Using a fork or a whisk, mix the peanut butter into the reserved broth until it is thoroughly blended. Stir in the sweet chili sauce, then pour the mixture into the skillet. Stir in the reserved noodles and simmer for two to three minutes, until the sauce thickens and the chicken is tender and no longer pink in the middle. Season with salt and pepper, and serve.

EASIEST PASTA

Makes 2 servings

*Convenience pastas are a close second to ramen
noodles when it comes to inexpensive, easy meals. Available
in many different flavors, they can be readily found in
almost any supermarket. If you take a little time to
add some extra ingredients, you can transform
a simple boxed pasta into a much
healthier and far tastier meal.*

1 tablespoon (15 ml) vegetable oil
1 tablespoon (15 ml) diced yellow onion

1 clove garlic, peeled and minced
1 large chicken breast, diced, about ½ cup (125 ml)
½ cup (125 ml) frozen mixed vegetables, thawed
1 4.6- to 5.3-ounce (130- to 150-g) package of side dish
  pasta, any flavor
⅔ cup (150 ml) milk (if called for in package directions)
⅔ cup (150 ml) water (if called for in package directions)
Salt and pepper, to taste

1. Heat the vegetable oil in a small saucepan over medium heat. When the oil is hot, add the onion and garlic and cook, stirring occasionally, for one minute or until the onion is translucent.

2. Add the chicken and cook, stirring occasionally, until the chicken is no longer pink on the outside.

3. Add the mixed vegetables and continue cooking and stirring for another minute or until the vegetables are tender.

4. Reduce the heat to low. Add the package of pasta along with the milk and water (if required). Simmer for five minutes or until the noodles are soft to the bite. Season with salt and pepper, if necessary, and serve.

Variations

1. Broccoli–Cheddar Pasta: Add ½ cup (125 ml) broccoli florets along with the pasta in step 4. Top the finished pasta with shredded Cheddar cheese.

2. Easy Pasta Alfredo: Add ½ cup (125 ml) diced mushrooms at the end of step 1. Cook for about two to three minutes, then proceed as directed. Top the finished pasta with 1 tablespoon (15 ml) freshly grated Parmesan cheese.

FAST PASTA

Makes 2 servings

*With some market-fresh vegetables, some pasta,
and a jar of prepared pasta sauce (any kind will do),
you can create a healthy meal in the time it takes to boil
the noodles. Have some fun exploring a market and talking
with the vendors, then enjoy this hearty pasta with a glass
of local red wine. Use any sauce that's left over on a
Pizza (in this chapter) or a Tuna-Veggie Melt (see
Sandwiches, Wraps, and Snacks) the next day.*

7 ounces (200 g) dried pasta such as fettuccini, spaghetti,
    rigatoni, etc.
2 tablespoons (30 ml) olive or canola oil
$\frac{1}{2}$ carrot, peeled and thinly sliced
2 tablespoons (30 ml) diced yellow onion
1 small clove of garlic, peeled and minced
1 green bell pepper, washed, seeded, and diced
6 mushrooms, washed and sliced
10 broccoli florets
1 cup (250 ml) tomato pasta sauce
Salt and pepper, to taste

1. Fill a large pot with water, add a dash of salt, and bring to
a boil over high heat.

2. Add the pasta and reduce the heat to medium, stirring
occasionally to prevent the pasta from sticking together.

3. While the pasta is cooking, heat the oil in a skillet over
medium heat. When the oil is hot, add the carrot, onion, and

garlic and cook, stirring occasionally, for about three to four minutes or until the onion is translucent.

4. Add the bell pepper and mushrooms and continue cooking and stirring until the mushrooms are juicy, about two minutes.

5. Add the broccoli and the tomato sauce and increase the heat to high. When the tomato sauce boils, reduce the heat to medium-low and simmer for two to three minutes or until the broccoli is tender. Season with salt and pepper.

6. When the pasta is tender to the bite, drain it in a colander and transfer the pasta to a large bowl. Top with the tomato sauce and serve.

Variation: Add a diced chicken breast to the skillet at the end of step 3. Cook, stirring occasionally, until the chicken is no longer pink on the outside. Proceed as directed.

PASTA OLIO

Makes 2 servings

This light and tasty olive oil–based pasta is especially good in summer when tomatoes are at their best. I recommend using very ripe tomatoes and a very nice extra-virgin olive oil. Seasoning generously with salt and pepper makes the flavors really pop. In Italy this recipe is traditionally made with just pasta, olive oil, and garlic, but I think this combination is a delicious one that adds some extra flavors.

1 tablespoon (15 ml) salt
12 ounces (340 g) linguine noodles
$\frac{1}{3}$ cup (75 ml) olive oil

2 tablespoons (30 ml) diced red onion
1 clove garlic, peeled and minced
$\frac{1}{2}$ teaspoon (2 ml) dried red pepper flakes (optional)
1 tomato, cut into bite-size chunks
8 kalamata olives (optional)
Salt and pepper, to taste
$\frac{1}{2}$ cup (125 ml) fresh spinach leaves

1. Fill a large pot with water. Add the salt and bring to a boil over high heat. Add the pasta, reduce the heat to medium, and simmer, stirring occasionally, until the pasta is tender to the bite. Drain in a colander and set aside.

2. Heat the oil in a skillet over medium heat. When the oil is hot, add the onion, garlic, and red pepper flakes (if using), and cook for one minute or until the onion is translucent but not browned.

3. Make sure the pasta in the colander is completely drained of water. Add the pasta to the skillet, along with the tomato and olives. Season well with salt and pepper and cook for one to two minutes until the pasta is heated through and is well coated with the oil.

4. Add the spinach and stir just until the spinach starts to wilt. Serve immediately.

Variations

1. Add $\frac{1}{2}$ cup (125 ml) diced chicken breast at the end of step 2. Cook the chicken, stirring occasionally, for three to five minutes or until the chicken is no longer pink in the middle. Proceed as directed.

2. Add any of these ingredients along with the pasta, tomato, and olives in step 3:

$^{1}/_{3}$ cup (75 ml) chopped sun-dried tomatoes
2 tablespoons (30 ml) pine nuts
4 anchovies, chopped
$^{1}/_{2}$ of a cooked Italian sausage link, sliced
$^{1}/_{4}$ cup (60 ml) sliced salami

PASTA BOLOGNESE

Makes 2 servings

I have vivid recollections of making this recipe with a group of friends in Byron Bay, Australia. It's a good recipe to prepare with a friend because one person can cook the noodles and the other person can cook the meat, then you both get to enjoy a hearty meal together. I strongly recommend that you purchase lean, not regular, ground beef. There is a significant difference in the amount of fat the meat releases when cooked. Using a prepared tomato pasta sauce adds extra flavor to this easy dish.

1 tablespoon (15 ml) salt
$^{1}/_{2}$ pound (227 g) dried pasta of any shape, such as
    spaghetti, fettuccini, penne, rigatoni, etc.
2 tablespoons (30 ml) olive oil or vegetable oil
$^{1}/_{2}$ cup (125 ml) finely diced yellow onion
3 tablespoons (45 ml) finely diced carrot
3 tablespoons (45 ml) finely diced celery
1 clove garlic, peeled and minced
$^{1}/_{2}$ pound (227 g) lean ground beef
2 tablespoons (30 ml) red wine (optional)
2 cups (500 ml) prepared tomato pasta sauce
Salt and pepper, to taste

1. Fill a large pot with water, add the salt, and bring to a boil over high heat. Add the pasta, reduce the heat to medium-low, and simmer, stirring occasionally, until the pasta is tender to the bite. Drain the pasta in a colander and set aside.

2. Heat the oil in a skillet over medium heat. When the oil is hot, add the onion, carrot, celery, and garlic. Cook, stirring occasionally, for two to three minutes or until the vegetables start to soften. Try not to brown them.

3. Add the ground beef to the skillet and cook, stirring occasionally, until the beef is well browned. Once the beef is cooked, pour off the fat into a bowl to discard later.

4. Stir in the red wine (if using) and pasta sauce and reduce the heat to low. Cook for about three to five more minutes or until the sauce reduces and thickens slightly. Season with salt and pepper, and serve.

Variations

1. Replace the ground beef with minced veal or chicken or with a vegetarian ground-beef substitute.

2. Add 5 mushrooms, sliced, to the skillet at the end of step 2 and cook, stirring occasionally, until the mushrooms are tender. Proceed as directed.

SPINACH–RICOTTA LASAGNA

Makes 6 to 8 servings

Lasagna is the perfect meal for a group or for the person who wants to cook only once and live on leftovers for a week. I find that when lasagna sits overnight in a refrigerator, the flavors blend so that it tastes even better the next day anyway. The most time-consuming part of making lasagna is the layering. It will go faster and be more fun if you make it with a friend or two.

2 eggs

1 15-ounce (425-g) container of ricotta cheese or cottage cheese

2 10-ounce (283-g) packages frozen chopped spinach, thawed and drained

$1/4$ cup (60 ml) grated Parmesan cheese

1 tablespoon (15 ml) dried basil

1 teaspoon (5 ml) garlic powder

1 teaspoon (5 ml) salt

1 teaspoon (5 ml) pepper

2 cups (500 ml) prepared tomato pasta sauce, divided

$1^1/2$ cups (375 ml) shredded mozzarella cheese, divided

9 oven-ready lasagna noodles (see Note)

1. Preheat the oven to 350°F (175°C). Lightly grease a 9-by-13-inch (23-by-33-cm) baking dish.

2. In a medium bowl, combine the eggs, ricotta or cottage cheese, spinach, Parmesan cheese, basil, garlic powder, salt, and pepper.

3. Pour $1/2$ cup (125 ml) of the pasta sauce into the greased baking dish and spread it with a spatula. Lay half the uncooked noodles over the sauce. Spread half the ricotta mixture over the noodles and sprinkle with a third of the mozzarella cheese. Repeat the layers, using another $1/2$ cup (125 ml) of the spaghetti sauce, the remaining half of the ricotta mixture, and another third of the mozzarella cheese.

4. Top with 1 cup (250 ml) of the spaghetti sauce and the remaining third of the mozzarella cheese.

5. Cover the baking dish securely with aluminum foil and bake in the preheated oven for one hour. Let stand 10 minutes before cutting and serving.

Note: If you can't find oven-ready lasagna noodles, purchase standard lasagna noodles. Prepare the noodles before continuing with the recipe: Bring a large pot of salted water to a boil. Add the noodles and cook for 8 to 10 minutes or until the noodles are tender to the bite. Drain in a colander and proceed with step 1.

Variation

Beef Lasagna: After step 1, heat 2 tablespoons (30 ml) vegetable oil in a skillet over medium heat. Add 1 pound (454 g) of lean ground beef to the skillet. Season with ½ teaspoon (2 ml) each of garlic powder, onion powder, salt, and pepper. Cook the beef, stirring occasionally, until it is browned, then add 1 cup (250 ml) of the pasta sauce. Bring to a simmer, then remove from the heat and let it cool.

Because of the addition of the beef, use half the ricotta mixture in step 2 above: Mix together 1 egg, 7 ounces (200 g) ricotta or cottage cheese, 1 package frozen spinach, and 2 tablespoons (30 ml) grated Parmesan cheese. Omit the dried basil, garlic powder, salt, and pepper because they're added to the beef mixture instead.

As in step 3, spread half the meat sauce in the baking dish. Lay half the uncooked noodles over the sauce. Top with the entire ricotta mixture and half the mozzarella cheese, then the rest of the noodles, then the remainder of the meat sauce and mozzarella cheese as in step 4. Bake as directed in step 5.

PIZZA

Makes two 12-inch (30-cm) pizzas

*It might seem crazy to make your own pizza dough
when you are traveling—especially if you never do it at home. But
trust me; this is so easy and so good. You can use a variety of herbs in
the dough: Italian mixed herbs, oregano, thyme, or rosemary. I created
this recipe in New Zealand when my friend Erin asked me if I could
give her a recipe for pizza dough because she wanted to make her
boyfriend a beautiful pizza when he arrived at the hostel. Drawing
on pizza dough recipes I had made in the past and with a little help
from a local chef, I came up with this dough. Erin made it and
loved it, and so did her boyfriend. Erin and her boyfriend are still
together, and Erin still has my pizza dough recipe.
Coincidence? I think not!*

Dough

2 cups (500 ml) all-purpose flour
1 cup (250 ml) whole-wheat flour
2 tablespoons (30 ml) dried basil
1 teaspoon (5 ml) garlic powder
1 teaspoon (5 ml) active dry yeast
1 teaspoon (5 ml) salt
1 cup (250 ml) warm water
2 tablespoons (30 ml) olive oil

Sauce and Topping Combinations

See combinations on the following pages. Layer ingredients
in the order listed.

1. Preheat the oven to 350°F (175°C).

2. In a mixing bowl, combine the flours, basil, garlic powder, yeast, and salt.

3. In a separate large mixing bowl, combine the water and olive oil.

4. Add half the flour mixture to the water mixture and mix well with a large wooden spoon or your hands; then add the rest of the flour mixture, mixing until combined.

5. Sprinkle a handful of flour on a clean work surface. Transfer the dough to the floured surface and knead for five to seven minutes or until the dough is smooth and elastic. If the dough sticks, sprinkle a little more flour on the work surface.

6. Roll the dough into a ball, place in a large bowl (leaving room for the dough to expand), cover with a cloth or plastic bag, and set aside in a warm spot to rise for about 45 minutes. (It should double in size.)

7. Remove the dough from the bowl and punch it down with a couple of hits. Shape it into another ball. Cut this ball in half and roll each half to 12 inches (30 cm) in diameter. Or wrap one ball of dough in plastic wrap and refrigerate it for up to three days.

8. Rub two baking sheets or pizza pans with olive oil. Slide the rolled-out dough onto the pans.

9. See below for pizza sauce and topping combinations. Spread sauce evenly over the dough. Sprinkle shredded cheese evenly over the sauce and add toppings. Bake for 15 to 20 minutes. If you bake both pizzas at once, use two oven racks. Watch the pizzas closely, rotating them occasionally so they cook evenly.

Note: If you're not keen on making your own pizza dough, try using pita bread. Add your sauce and toppings and simply bake it in a toaster oven or broil it in a regular oven until the cheese is melted.

Dough Variation

To make a simpler pizza dough, omit the whole-wheat flour and use 3 cups (750 ml) of all-purpose flour. Omit the garlic powder and dried basil and proceed as directed.

Combo Pizza

1 cup (250 ml) tomato sauce

2 to 4 mushrooms, washed and sliced

2 tablespoons (30 ml) chopped green onion

2 ounces (63 g) pepperoni, about 4 or 5 slices

1½ cups (375 ml) shredded mozzarella cheese

Pesto Pizza

1 cup (250 ml) prepared pesto sauce

½ cup (125 ml) Basic Sautéed Chicken (see Sandwiches, Wraps, and Snacks)

½ cup (125 ml) diced bell pepper

½ cup (125 ml) diced tomato

½ cup (125 ml) shredded mozzarella cheese

3 tablespoons (45 ml) grated Parmesan cheese

Barbecue Pizza

1 cup (250 ml) barbecue sauce

½ cup (125 ml) Basic Sautéed Chicken (see Sandwiches, Wraps, and Snacks)

¼ cup (60 ml) diced red onion

½ cup (125 ml) pineapple chunks

1 cup (250 ml) shredded Gouda cheese

Rustic Pizza

⅓ cup (75 ml) olive oil

½ teaspoon (2 ml) dried basil

½ teaspoon (2 ml) dried oregano

½ cup (125 ml) sliced tomato

½ cup (125 ml) diced asparagus, steamed or parboiled

8 to 10 kalamata olives

1 cup (250 ml) shredded mozzarella cheese

Salt and pepper, to taste

RATATOUILLE

Makes 2 to 3 servings

*There is no greater recipe for market-fresh
vegetables than ratatouille. This Mediterranean dish really
brings out the natural flavors of fresh vegetables and herbs.
If you have the luck of being close to a farmers market,
take this recipe with you and look for the ingredients there.
You will get more out of your cooking when you put this kind
of effort into it. I usually eat ratatouille with fresh,
warm Italian bread, but you can also serve it over
Basic Rice or Garlic Smashed Potatoes
(see Salads and Side Dishes).*

3 tablespoons (45 ml) olive oil

½ cup (125 ml) chopped red onion

2 cloves garlic, peeled and minced

¹/₂ cup (125 ml) stemmed and cubed eggplant

¹/₂ cup (125 ml) cubed zucchini

¹/₂ cup (125 ml) chopped seeded green bell pepper

¹/₂ cup (125 ml) coarsely chopped tomato

¹/₄ cup (60 ml) sliced black olives (optional)

2 teaspoons (10 ml) dried basil

2 teaspoons (10 ml) dried oregano

Salt and pepper, to taste

1. Heat the olive oil in a medium-size saucepan over medium-high heat. When the oil is hot, add the onion and garlic and cook, stirring occasionally, for two to three minutes or until the onion is translucent.

2. Add the eggplant, zucchini, and bell pepper and cook, stirring occasionally, for two to three minutes or until the vegetables begin to soften.

3. Stir in the tomato, olives (if using), basil, and oregano and continue cooking until the mixture is thoroughly heated. Season with salt and pepper, and serve.

Variations

1. Chicken Ratatouille: Add one diced chicken breast after you sauté the onions and garlic in step 1. Cook the chicken, stirring occasionally, for about 2 minutes, or until the chicken is lightly browned and no longer pink in the middle, then proceed as directed.

2. Tofu Ratatouille: Add 1 cup (250 ml) diced extra-firm tofu along with the eggplant and other vegetables in step 2. Proceed as directed.

RISOTTO

Makes 2 main-dish servings or 3 side-dish servings

*Risotto is made with an Italian rice called
arborio rice. It requires a little more effort to make than
regular rice, but the end product is a fantastic, creamy delight!
The keys to successful risotto are adding the liquid a
small amount at a time, stirring constantly, and
making sure the rice absorbs most of the
liquid before you add more.*

3 tablespoons (45 ml) vegetable oil or butter
$\frac{1}{2}$ cup (125 ml) finely diced yellow onion, about $\frac{1}{2}$ large
onion
1 tablespoon (15 ml) chopped garlic, about 2 cloves
1 cup (250 ml) arborio rice
3 cups (750 ml) chicken stock, vegetable stock, or water,
warmed in a saucepan or microwave
$\frac{1}{2}$ cup (125 ml) grated Parmesan cheese
Salt and pepper, to taste

1. Heat the vegetable oil or butter in a large saucepan over medium-high heat.

2. When the oil is hot, add the onion and garlic and cook, stirring occasionally, for three to four minutes or until the onion is translucent. Do not brown.

3. Stir in the rice and reduce the heat to medium. Cook the rice for about two minutes, stirring occasionally, until the rice starts absorbing the oil.

4. Slowly add 1 cup (250 ml) of warm stock or water. Stir

constantly until most of the liquid is absorbed. Then add 1 more cup of the liquid and repeat until you use all the liquid or until the risotto is creamy (not runny) and soft to the bite. This should take about 20 minutes.

5. Stir in the Parmesan cheese, season with salt and pepper, and serve immediately.

Variations

1. At the end of step 2, stir in ½ cup (125 ml) diced button mushrooms, or any other diced vegetable, and cook for two to three minutes or until the mushrooms or other vegetables start to soften. Proceed as directed.

2. Or add ½ cup (125 ml) frozen vegetables after you have added almost all the stock in step 4. This will heat the vegetables through but won't overcook them.

Sweet Treats

BANANA RICE PUDDING

Makes 2 servings

This recipe is a variation on a banana–coconut milk dessert I learned to make while I was in Thailand. It's a light, healthy, and refreshing summer treat and an easy way to use leftover cooked rice (even over-cooked rice). Coconut milk can be found in most supermarkets, usually in the Asian foods section or near the stir-fry section.

1 14-ounce (400 ml) can coconut milk

2 cups (500 ml) cooked white rice or Basic Rice (see Salads and Side Dishes)

1 large ripe banana, peeled and chopped, about 1 cup (250 ml)

2 tablespoons (30 ml) honey

1. Place the coconut milk, rice, and banana in a small saucepan and bring to a boil over medium-high heat, stirring occasionally.

2. Once the mixture comes to a boil, continue boiling, stirring occasionally, for one minute. Remove from the heat and stir in the honey.

3. Pour the mixture into a bowl and cool in the refrigerator for one to two hours or until it sets.

Variations

1. Add 1 teaspoon (5 ml) ginger powder along with the honey in step 2.

2. Add ½ teaspoon (2 ml) vanilla essence or vanilla extract along with the honey in step 2.

CRÊPES

Makes 2 to 3 crêpes

*Crêpes can be a refreshing breakfast or a beautiful,
light dessert. Plain fruit topped with yogurt is nice, but wrap the
fruit in a crêpe and it instantly becomes a sexy creation. Top it off
with a couple dollops of your favorite yogurt, and it is downright
beautiful. I suggest making this recipe for a loved one or a certain
crush you're trying to impress. It's sure to melt some hearts.*

Crêpes

2 eggs
³/₄ cup (175 ml) milk
²/₃ cup (150 ml) all-purpose flour
1 teaspoon (5 ml) granulated sugar
¹/₂ teaspoon (2 ml) salt
1 tablespoon (15 ml) vegetable oil, plus 2 to 3 teaspoons
    (10 to 15 ml) for cooking

Filling

¹/₂ cup (125 ml) fresh or canned strawberries
or
¹/₂ cup (125 ml) mixed fruit, such as blueberries,
    raspberries, cantaloupe, and kiwi fruit

Topping

2 tablespoons (30 ml) strawberry yogurt

1. In a bowl, combine the eggs, milk, flour, sugar, salt, and 1 tablespoon (15 ml) of the vegetable oil. Whisk until smooth.

2. Heat a nonstick skillet over medium-high heat. Add 1 teaspoon (5 ml) of the vegetable oil and wipe it around the pan with a paper towel to coat the entire surface.

3. Pour $\frac{1}{4}$ cup (60 ml) of the crêpe batter into the pan, tilting the pan to completely coat the pan's surface with the batter. Cook the crêpe on the first side for two to three minutes or until golden. Flip it and cook the second side an additional one to two minutes or until golden brown. Transfer the crêpe to a plate and repeat with the remaining batter, oiling the pan again for each crêpe.

4. Place a spoonful of filling down the center of each crêpe. Fold the crêpe over the filling, top with the yogurt, and serve immediately.

VOLUME MEASURES
(Approximate)

UTENSIL MEASURE	OUNCE MEASURE	METRIC EQUIVALENT
¼ teaspoon		1 ml
½ teaspoon		2 ml
¾ teaspoon		4 ml
1 teaspoon		5 ml
1 tablespoon	.5 fl ounce	15 ml
1½ tablespoons	.75 fl ounce	20 ml
2 tablespoons	1 fl ounce	30 ml
¼ cup (4T)	2 fl ounces	60 ml
⅓ cup	3 flounces	75 ml
½ cup	4 fl ounces	125 ml
⅔ cup	5 fl ounces	150 ml
¾ cup	6 fl ounces	175 ml
1 cup	8 fl ounces	250 ml
2 cups	16 fl ounces	500 ml

Less than ¼ teaspoon is a "pinch" for dry ingredients and a "dash" for liquid.

WEIGHT MEASURES
(Approximate)

¼ lb (4 ounces)	125 g
½ lb (8 ounces)	250 g
1 lb	500 g
2 lbs	1 kg
3 lb	1.5 kg
4 lb	2 kg

ABOUT THE AUTHOR

Mike Hedley is a Canadian-rated "Red Seal" chef and an experienced backpacking traveler. Beginning in 2002, he spent twenty-six months traveling through Australia, New Zealand, Thailand, and Germany. He is currently a cooking instructor and is actively planning his next epic adventure. He lives in Winnipeg, Manitoba, Canada.

INDEX

THE MOUNTAINEERS, founded in 1906, is a nonprofit outdoor activity and conservation club whose mission is "to explore, study, preserve, and enjoy the natural beauty of the outdoors. . . ." Based in Seattle, Washington, the club is now the third-largest such organization in the United States, with seven branches throughout Washington State.

The Mountaineers sponsors both classes and year-round outdoor activities in the Pacific Northwest, which include hiking, mountain climbing, ski-touring, snowshoeing, bicycling, camping, kayaking, nature study, sailing, and adventure travel. The club's conservation division supports environmental causes through educational activities, sponsoring legislation, and presenting informational programs.

All club activities are led by skilled, experienced instructors who are dedicated to promoting safe and responsible enjoyment and preservation of the outdoors.

If you would like to participate in these organized outdoor activities or the club's programs, consider a membership in The Mountaineers. For information and an application, write or call The Mountaineers, Club Headquarters, 300 Third Avenue West, Seattle, WA 98119; 206-284-6310. You can also visit the club's website at *www.mountaineers.org* or contact The Mountaineers via email at clubmail@mountaineers.org.

The Mountaineers Books, an active, nonprofit publishing program of the club, produces guidebooks, instructional texts, historical works, natural history guides, and works on environmental conservation. All books produced by The Mountaineers Books fulfill the club's mission.

Send or call for our catalog of more than 500 outdoor titles:
The Mountaineers Books
1001 SW Klickitat Way, Suite 201
Seattle, WA 98134
800-553-4453
mbooks@mountaineersbooks.org
www.mountaineersbooks.org

The Mountaineers Books is proud to be a corporate sponsor of The Leave No Trace Center for Outdoor Ethics, whose mission is to promote and inspire responsible outdoor recreation through education, research, and partnerships. The Leave No Trace program is focused specifically on human-powered (non-motorized) recreation.

Leave No Trace strives to educate visitors about the nature of their recreational impacts, as well as offer techniques to prevent and minimize such impacts. Leave No Trace is best understood as an educational and ethical program, not as a set of rules and regulations.

OTHER TITLES YOU MIGHT ENJOY FROM THE MOUNTAINEERS BOOKS

Beyond Gorp: Favorite Foods from Outdoor Experts
Yvonne Prater and Ruth Dyar Mendenhall
Outdoor experts, celebrities, and industry leaders share their favorite trail recipes.

Digital Photography Outdoors: A Field Guide for Adventure and Travel
James Martin
Special digital techniques for outdoor adventure shooting.

The Pocket Doctor: A Passport to Healthy Travel, 3rd Edition
Stephen Bezruchka, M.D.
Pocket-sized advice for staying healthy during international travels.

Backcountry Cooking: From Pack to Plate in 10 Minutes
Dorcas Miller
More than 144 recipes and how to plan simple meals.

Adventure Journal
Kristen Hostetter
Inspiration and a perfect format for chronicling your outdoor adventures.
